# PLUS

# PLUS
# jestico + whiles

Artifice
books on architecture

# Contents

PLUS
jestico + whiles

# Foreword

It is difficult to visualise a typical Jestico + Whiles building. They do not have a house style, yet their buildings are consistently powerful in their presence and in their look. When I attempt to recall an example, the British Council's building in Prague of 1992 flashes on that inward eye. The simple gridded glass interior of the refurbished 1920s structure simultaneously reflects the history of the original building while presenting a modern and forward-looking image for the Council.

Leap ahead a couple of decades and the W Hotel in Leicester Square with its sheer glazed facade comes to mind, its changing light display creating a strong presence on a key site in the heart of London's entertainment district. Pulsating by night; more modest by day.

Between these two contrasting projects is a portfolio of work that covers a wide range of building types—education and health, residential and retail, restaurants and racetracks—some buildings of serious social purpose, others for culture, leisure and entertainment, but all carried out with clean contemporary lines that reflect the practice's consistency of thinking and its pragmatic approach to design.

In an era when we are beset by huge inequalities of wealth and opportunity, when iconic towers overshadow areas of deprivation, one feels that Jestico + Whiles are a practice that has been able to hold onto the enduring values of an architectural practice that provides real benefit to society.

They run the firm in a way that reflects the importance of the people in it. They operate from a quiet cul-de-sac in Camden that is nevertheless very central. They are a modest bunch, yet keen to tell the world of their achievement through books like this or their informative newsletters. They are a practice that seems to have achieved an enviable balance in what they do.

In one newsletter director Heinz Richardson is photographed next to a quotation which says "Design for life, not for magazine covers!" This to me summed up not only the problem of much architecture today, but the essential common sense and thoughtfulness that Jestico + Whiles bring to the day-to-day practise of architecture—a social art that can help to create better lives, husband scarce resources but can also deliver delight and fun.

**Peter Murray, Chairman NLA: London's Centre for the Built Environment**

Practice

(Incr)Edible Footbridge
In December 2010, people at J+W gave
up designing schools, hotels and labs
for half a day and instead recreated the
Millennium Bridge in raw vegetables.
Similarly outlandish Practice Half Days
are staged every month.

# Practice

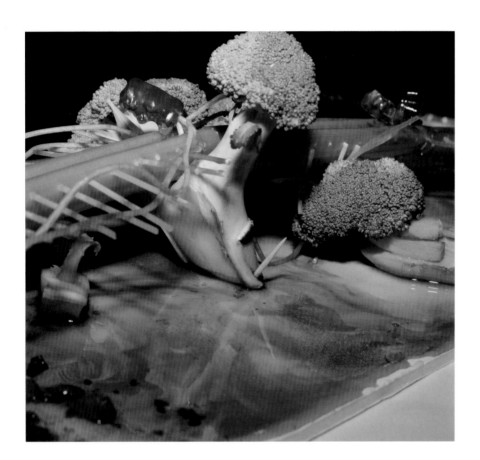

Now in its 35th year, Jestico + Whiles has entered the ranks
of the top 40 largest architectural practices in the *Architects'
Journal*'s 2012 survey. And the practice continues to grow in
their London and Prague offices where they have won over
160 awards and commendations for their work.

In truth, the practice was not launched in 1977 with a
heroic vision of an architectural powerhouse that would

endure and expand over several decades. It was more a
matter of the gradual drifting together of two self-employed
architects made redundant in a recession.

Between 1977 and 1979, Tom Jestico and John Whiles
rented desks opposite each other in shared office space
in Covent Garden. Though they had never actually worked
together before, they both came from the same stable, the
then Farrell Grimshaw Partnership

While still self-employed, they occasionally shared small
conversion projects. In fact, the name Jestico + Whiles
was first coined to indicate two freelancers working
together on the same project, and the plus sign has stuck
ever since.

It was John Whiles' accountant who came up with the idea
of a formal partnership. Whiles recalls: "He said: 'If you're
sharing some work between you, why not formalise this
and share all your work?'"

Once established, the practice had an uncanny knack of
picking up not just new building projects but whole new
development sectors. It did so by being alert and reacting
nimbly and intelligently to unanticipated events in the world
at large in what Whiles calls an open-minded approach. As
a rule, J+W made such a good fist of its first project in a
new sector that it became an acknowledged expert in that
sector. By these means, the practice has over the years
built up track records and client bases in an exceptionally
wide spectrum of development sectors.

A case in point happened in 1991, two years after the fall of
the Berlin Wall, when the practice was asked by a third party
to appraise a state department of architecture in Hungary.
The British Council got wind of this, mistakenly thought

In starchitects' footsteps
A visit to Rem Koolhaas's Casa de Musica
in Porto was the highlight of 2008's annual
study trip to architecturally distinguished
cities in Europe.

Practice

11

Western developers' subsequent incursions into the newly liberated Eastern Europe.

Right from the start, the two founders resolved to be more supportive of staff than they themselves had been when they were summarily made redundant by former employers. By 2000, they also wanted to promote a younger generation to director level, which would have required the latter buying a substantial stake in the company. But the value of the company, they then discovered, had escalated to a level that put the affordability of such a succession out of reach. In 2001, the company accountant came up with a solution to this succession impasse that would at the same time benefit all the staff. This was for the entire equity of the company to be transferred to an employee benefit trust, on similar lines to the John Lewis Partnership.

So where does 35 years of growth and evolution leave J+W in 2012? What makes the practice tick? And what marks it out from other architects? Perhaps the best way of answering these questions is to think of J+W as a trinity or triangle made up of the practice organisation, its members and their architectural output. This triangular relationship is inherently more robust than the crude push-pull line of supply and demand that typically connects architects with their clients.

that J+W had established itself in Hungary, and invited it to bid for new centres in Budapest and Prague. Fortunately at the same time the practice had just sponsored 15 Czech students' first visit to London and in so doing established a friendship that led J+W to become very knowledgeable with architecture and construction in Prague. The British Council's resulting commission for their new cultural centre in the city put the practice in a strong position to benefit from the

Much more than that, the three lines that connect the organisation of J+W, its members and their output can be regarded as thick bonds or cords made of at least ten strands. As spelled out below, these strands vary in nature from hard professional production (Strands 1, 3, 4, 5, 6 and 10) to a caring/sharing relationship (Strand 2), while others can appear downright facetious and pranky (Strands 7, 8 and 9). The really remarkable thing is that all ten strands are intertwined so that they reinforce each other, and they all pull

**Not wood but steel**
An early example of artificially rusted
Corten steel was spotted on a study
trip to Bregenz in 2008 and has since
become a J+W favourite.

both ways for the benefit of all three participants. It all adds up to a three-way bond that is truly mutual, robust, benign and—yes—unique.

### Strand 1: Diversity of development sectors
J+W has over the years built up, and still maintains, a diversity of work that is the envy of practices of similar, upper-middle-ranking size. As displayed in this book's nine succeeding chapters, projects range from low-budget building conversions (Interventions) to City financial head offices (Working), and from luxury apartments to new ways of integrating older people into their inner-city community (Living), plus a sprinkling of cutting-edge, one-off houses (Living and Plus). Other sectors tackled by the practice stretch from schools for disadvantaged children to university departments (Learning), and from five-star hotels and their interiors (Theatre and Interventions) to city-centre railway viaducts (Progress).

Geographically, work now extends right across Europe into Russia, much of it carried out in the Prague office. And beyond Russia, projects stretch out to the Middle East, India and as far as China and Australia. In hard times, such as the present recession, this wide spectrum of work is a lifeline. Currently, as commercial and school commissions in the UK tail off, they are replaced by increasing work in housing. And outside the troubled developed world, hotel and cinema building in India is still going strong.

The directors have not forgotten the lesson of how they had initially picked up work in all these sectors and regions. "It's all about taking advantage of things when they arise", says Tom Jestico. "And being able to leap on them and go with them."

### Strand 2: Employee Benefit Trust
After one year of service all staff automatically become members of the Employee Benefit Trust that owns the

**Pasta's golden glow**
A must-have pendant lamp was assembled
out of lasagna sheets, balsa wood and paper
clips, all found lying around the office, in a
Practice Half Day in February 2012.

A shelter for the weather
A rustic meteorological station caught
the eye and pen of Tom Jestico while on
a study trip to Lisbon in 2005.

systems, practical design and production information, and guides to external information sources and the thickets of statutory requirements and codes, all compiled in-house. The intranet takes the form of an extensive, interactive compendium of matrices, which invite users to click their way through a wide range of topics and then down into several layers of increasingly detailed, specialist information. In total, J+W's intranet provides all the information needed for basic building and interior design, but at a high level of professional competence and in a very accessible and clearly laid out manner. And as a bonus, it can deliver marketing displays for all 15 of J+W's development sectors, each presented as a matrix full of the practice's most dazzling projects.

### Strand 4: Directors as design champions

Tony Ling, Heinz Richardson and John Whiles, the three architect directors, and Tom Jestico, now acting as a senior consultant, all cast themselves as design champions. They constantly exhort all their colleagues to raise their game and aim for more inspired designs.

"The intranet is the hard stuff, and using it doesn't guarantee that the design is going to be brilliant", says Richardson. "The softer stuff we're very mindful of is always to strive to achieve better and higher quality design. It's always about questioning whether or not we can get something fresh out of a project that we haven't got before."

The directors repeatedly stress that, to them, higher quality design means avoiding elaborate stylistics in favour of architecture that is simple, rational, contemporary, pragmatic and cost-effective.

In championing good design, they brandish more carrot than stick, and more infectious enthusiasm than carrot. "We

whole company. As such people can be expected to be more loyal to the practice and work harder for it, particularly since all the distributable profits are paid as bonuses to Trust members every year. The bonus payment is based on a special system that has been devised whereby members are marked on ten aspects of performance and their final score determines their reward, irrespective of their position in the practice.

As well as providing compelling work incentives, the trust and its bonus schemes enshrine a strong egalitarianism that underpins the company and the convivial, approachable ethos of its staff that many people remark on. The caring/sharing trust is also reflected in five good employer awards and commendations that the firm has won over the last six years.

### Strand 3: Intranet matrices

Like many architects, the practice has set up its own intranet as an information resource for staff, as is encouraged by the quality assurance code, ISO 9001, under which it is certified. Yet J+W has expanded and intensified its intranet into a digital Aladdin's cave bursting with practice management

Scenery on a larger scale fascinated
senior architect Gail Ross on the same
study trip to Lisbon.

Fishy flood defence
The Thames Barrier was reconstructed
in smoked fish on the Practice Half Day
devoted to (Incr)Edible Architecture in
December 2010.

simply enjoy design", says John Whiles. "And we love to share our enthusiasm by creating great working relationships and buildings of excellence and enduring quality."

### Strand 5: Sustainability Plans and Green Team

Right from its early industrial buildings of the 1970s, the practice has taken delight in ingenious technical fixes and a quasi-engineering approach to architectural design. This technical expertise quickly migrated into low-energy design and from there into full-blown and frequently pioneering sustainable design—as Richardson says, "well before it became mainstream".

Yet for a practice that is loosely split into studios focused on various sectors, there is no sustainability studio—and no sustainability chapter in this book. That is because sustainable design permeates all projects, on a par with cost and aesthetics. And a Green Team has been set up with representatives from every studio to champion green issues. The Green Team assigns a 'Sustainability Plan' to each project, develops new initiatives and compiles and regularly updates a sheaf of highly informative sustainability matrices on the practice intranet (Strand 4).

The practice is certified under the international environmental management standard, ISO 14001, and last year it was selected as one of *The Sunday Times* 60 best green companies.

### Strand 6: Regular project design reviews

To help boost design quality, every project in the practice is intensively reviewed in three types of design reviews. All-round design reviews are chaired by a director and carried out at key stages such as feasibility study, planning application and contract tendering. Sustainability reviews are conducted by the Green Team, likewise at key stages. And, for projects at detailed design stage, reviews of fabric, structure, services and construction are conducted by the practice's Technical Team. All reviews are documented for future reference.

### Strand 7: Monthly Beer Busts

Beer Busts involve—you've guessed it—drinking beer. They are office social occasions held every month in the reception area. Beer Busts also have a serious purpose, conducted in an intentionally relaxed atmosphere. "We bring out the TV on wheels from the other room, and we ask groups to present their projects to the whole office", explains Richardson. "Not directors or associate directors but people on the team who might not normally be used to public speaking. It gives them the opportunity to present their work and to improve their communication skills. And it keeps everyone in the organisation up to speed with what we're all doing."

"In the Beer Busts, we try to instil enthusiasm, lateral thinking and cross-fertilisation from one studio to another", continues Richardson. "For instance, the interior design studio might be doing the most amazing hotel interiors in India or Leicester Square. That might then inform the interior design of a school, where the budgets are very different."

### Strand 8: Monthly Practice Half Days

Once a month, the whole office takes half a day off real work to participate in extracurricular activities, followed by a practice lunch. Practice Half Days (PHDs) are organised by the senior architects, who devise unexpected, often outlandish events to jolt their colleagues to think outside the box and to foster good-humoured team spirit. Themes for PHDs have included (Incr)Edible Architecture, which produced Canary Wharf Tower out of toast and London Eye in pastry and marshmallows. On another occasion, 11 senior staff sashayed down an impromptu catwalk in Regent's Park masquerading as the Sydney Opera House, the Eiffel Tower and other global icons. They had been kitted out by groups of six earlier in the day. As John Whiles comments,

**The fish that earned its stripes**
A fish was first photographed and later
given a stripey new overcoat on a Practice
Half Day in May 2012 devoted to improving
Photoshop skills.

Practice

17

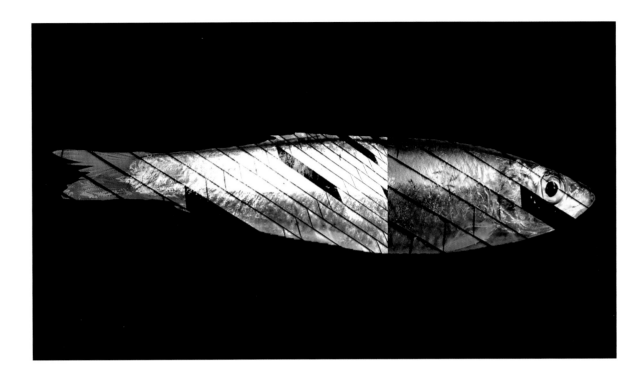

"PHDs keep ideas and creativity flowing so that the practice remains fresh and innovative."

### Strand 9: Study trips
Yearly study trips, typically to architecturally distinguished European cities, are popular staff perks at J+W. The adventurous spirit of study trips is usually heightened by pranky false leads or riddles in the invitation. In 1997, for instance, a coach trip was laid on to Niels Torp's newly completed BA Headquarters in Harmondsworth. But the coach turned unexpectedly into Heathrow Airport nearby, and the group was whisked off instead for a weekend in Bilbao and visit to Frank Gehry's newly opened Guggenheim. People were issued with boxer shorts, T-shirts and their own clandestinely obtained passports. And just like other J+W fun events, these foreign jaunts have a serious underlying message. "They are to tell people here that there are other ways of doing things", says John Whiles. "As the practice develops more and more abroad, we shouldn't always think in English ways."

### Strand 10: Dialogue with each other and the world at large
The practice markets itself conscientiously, as is evident in the awards and commendations that the practice has won and the constant stream of journal articles and other media coverage. The task of marketing is made lighter by the innate openness, approachability and friendliness of the entire practice. Staff are kept in the publicity loop by a large noticeboard in reception where articles are displayed. They are also encouraged to swap project images and information among themselves by another noticeboard in reception, a regular newsletter, the practice intranet (Strand 3) and the monthly Beer Busts (Strand 7).

At the age of 35, J+W is larger than ever, despite the recession. As a general rule, when founders hand over the reins of their business, their guiding vision departs with them. In architectural practices, the typical pattern is for its designs to lose their edge and become more commercial and corporate. As its ten intertwined strands show, however, J+W shows no signs at all of any loss of vision or weakening grip. Everything it says and does points to an architectural practice in rude health and enthusiastically supported by everyone working for it.

Long may this continue!

# Profiles:
# Jestico + Whiles' founding
# and current directors

## Tom Jestico

Tom Jestico describes himself as a practical nuts-and-bolts designer. He delights in getting his hands dirty constructing and restoring buildings, aircraft and cars. He also has a perennial *joie de vivre* that is infectious.

Born in 1942, he grew up in the village of Great Shelford south of Cambridge. As a schoolboy, he set his heart on becoming an RAF pilot, but fluffed the interview. Instead he attended the foundation course at Cambridge School of Art. One day, he was taken by a tutor on a group bicycle ride round Cambridge. "It turned a switch on in my head", he recalls. "I thought: 'This is

fantastic. I want to be an architect.'" He then studied architecture on the traditional route while working in an architect's office and finished his course full-time in Birmingham.

While running his architecture practice, Jestico has also found the time and energy to co-write an architectural guide to London, build a microlight aircraft, restore a classic Alfa Romeo car, build two new houses and refurbish another. Though now semi-retired, he is "still flying on average once a fortnight and about to embark on another kit plane with a friend".

## John Whiles

John Whiles takes an intellectual, conceptual approach to architecture. As well as being a raconteur with a dry wit, he likes to invoke abstract terms such as rationalist, logical, contextual and geometric.

Born in 1947, he grew up in the well-heeled London suburb of Richmond on the flight path to London airport. As a schoolboy, he aspired to run a commercial airline. But in a job interview at British European Airways, he was advised to go to university first and to study architecture. He then attended the avant-garde Architectural Association School of Architecture, where he fell under the spell of three Greek tutors. "I had grown up in London and come through the English school system, and they opened my eyes to a much wider perspective", he says.

The Greeks also urged Whiles to travel the globe and work in offices in New York, South America and Australia "some 25 years before the invention of 'gap years'". That same wanderlust has since led him to kayaking down the Zambesi, traversing the central Australian desert and motorbiking around South America. He has also won medals in European swimming championships "for people of certain ages".

# Heinz Richardson

Right from the age of ten, Heinz Richardson knew that he wanted to be an architect. Born in Germany, he spent his formative years on a farm in Yorkshire, helping his father mend fences, make rabbit hutches and generally living and loving the outdoor life. This period may have fired not only his enthusiasm for building, but for the environment, both of which have been enduring passions.

After passing his 11-plus examination he is thankful for having the chance to attend grammar school. The headmistress of his primary school spotted his love of buildings and gave him a history of architecture guide as a leaving present. He read it avidly, and spent long days travelling and sketching buildings. Having graduated from the Bartlett School of Architecture in the recession of 1975 he had spells with Sheppard Robson and formed a practice which he ran with two others, before joining Jestico + Whiles in 1986. If pushed, he describes himself as a 'green modernist' interested in designing architecture that puts people first, but with delight as an important extra. Heinz has designed a number of innovative low-energy projects, including the ground-breaking Zero-Energy Office for Hyndburn Borough Council and the House for the Future at the Museum of Welsh Life. Education projects also hold a particular interest because, delivered with skill, they provide the impetus for careers Heinz himself has enjoyed.

A keen follower of cricket and football—Richardson played for Buckinghamshire when at school—he also enjoys travelling and absorbing different cultures. Now 58, he says he will only begin to think of retirement when he doesn't look forward to work, and going into the office. "I have no regrets", he says. "I love life and the people who surround me."

## Tony Ling

58-year-old Tony Ling describes himself as a "knowledge-phile" who enjoys the "friendly, generous and competent atmosphere" of the Jestico + Whiles office and the varied work he is involved with.

Born in Hong Kong, he emigrated with his parents, settling in London—in Canada. He strove to pursue a fine art degree at Waterloo University, somewhat against the wishes of his parents, who put a greater stall on more vocational choices, but settled on engineering ("boring"), then transferred to architecture after discovering its attractions via his then housemates. Following graduation, and a period working on residential, offices and even theme parks at commercial practices in Toronto, Canada, the then married Ling moved to the UK, where he joined J+W in 1989. After a one-and-a-half year break in Paris with his musician wife, he returned and became a director in 2008. "I'm definitely interested in the functional side of architecture", he says. "I want to make spaces that do what they're asked to do, but which also offer delight and wit."

Ling has worked on a number of key projects for the practice, such as Borough Market and the highly technical, award-winning Mountbatten Building in Southampton, and is currently working on the Graphene Laboratory Building project in Manchester. A part-time tutor at the Bartlett School of Architecture and visiting critic at the Architectural Association, Ling enjoys reading, all forms of music, visiting galleries and satiating his thirst for knowledge in history, religion and other issues, both off and online.

## Suzanne Gilmour

Suzanne Gilmour was born in 1956 in Harare, Zimbabwe where she completed her schooling, after which at her parents' suggestion she went to England for a year and completed a business diploma. Intending to return to Zimbabwe and go to university, she instead got a job in the library at what was then the University of Rhodesia, from where she transferred to the Geology Department as a technician. After meeting her husband, the pair took off travelling for four years at the end of the 'hippy' 70s. "We lived a pretty peripatetic life, working only when we needed money", she says. Following her country's independence Gilmour returned to work in the R&D department of one of Zimbabwe's breweries before spending three years in Mogadishu, Somalia, working for USAID and the International Committee of the Red Cross.

In late 1987 she came to England intending to stay only for a couple of years, choosing Jestico + Whiles over the Institute of

Directors "because they were so welcoming and informal and I liked the idea of working in a creative environment", and because the staff clearly felt her myriad of jobs was a plus point. The directors gave Gilmour the freedom to develop her own role, changing it as the practice evolved. As a director today she runs the day-to-day business of the practice including the support side, finance and human resources.

Now living on the riverside in Kingston upon Thames, Gilmour's interests include her lifelong passion for horses and producing olive oil from their quinta in Central Portugal.

# Beginnings

26

PLUS
jestico + whiles

Policy Studies Institute, Camden, 1984
Green shoots: An early, low energy
conversion of a wedge-shaped block in
Camden's Park Village East in London.

# Beginnings

The myriad conversions Jestico + Whiles undertook in its early years—primarily of houses into flats, perhaps around five a year, and mainly in north London—proved to be a useful primer, and a familiar way into the practice of architecture. John Whiles recalls how these 25 or so schemes for private clients and developers, many of them elicited from friends or friends-of-friends, taught the fledgling firm an understanding of how to integrate services, spatial and fire requirements—all those things which were needed but without the worry of structure, envelope and planning.

One of the bigger of these schemes was Ransomes Dock, the conversion of an old ice factory, then cold store, in Parkgate Road, Battersea. Swiss entrepreneur Carlo Gatti, the man credited with bringing ice cream to the world, owned the original building. With the aid of a £430,000 Urban Development Grant, which was much trumpeted by the Conservative Government of the time, this was to be converted into flexible workspaces—an early marker in this trend. The project emerged from a serendipitous call from a family friend of Whiles', developer Paul Cook, who kept the top floor of the completed conversion of offices as his loft apartment. Such conversions were providing the practice not only with a crucial flow of steady work, but also, in retrospect, a kind of liberty for the architects. "It gave you a freedom to design", recalls Whiles. "Some people say that much of the best British architecture is done between party walls and that English architects are not always at their best on totally open greenfield sites."

Ransomes Dock, and many like it in this period between 1975 and 1982, also served to teach the firm early lessons about contracts, says Jestico, about the kinds of relationships that occur between clients and builders, and sometimes for the architect to detail the elements of the building that matter to them, and leave the rest to the builder. Conversions were also, of course, all the rage, with many making a lot of money out of the process, converting houses into flats.

The Policy Studies Institute was another conversion, this time of a wedge-shaped building overlooking the railway lines leading out of Euston Station at Park Village East in Camden. This was 1983, and the Green architecture movement was beginning to bubble away in the background, so the project attained an environmentally conscious flavour. The existing building was a dismal office block and its difficult shape—a wedge tapering from 25 metres to virtually nothing—meant a large part of the interior was unusable as cellular office space, the client's preference. J+W chose to knock out the centre of the scheme's tight triangle, installing a glazed atrium running through three of the five floors, and grouping the 64 small offices around it. The ductwork 'sucked' the hot air building up at the top of the atrium and blew warm air out to heat the lower levels.

Alongside Tom Jestico's own new build house that he
completed in Greenwich in 1973, two notable industrial
projects joined the residential and office conversions to form
a key part in the practice's workload and reputation: one in
Epsom—see Case Study—and the other in Waltham Cross.
The former was on a prime site near the entrance to the
Local Authority-owned Epsom Industrial Estate for which the
District Council was keen to see an exemplar development.
The original architects who had obtained permission for a
typical asbestos 'shed', had recently retired, opening up the
opportunity for John Whiles' father, a consultant surveyor, to
suggest using the now named, Jestico + Whiles Architects to
complete the work. Fortunately the developer accepted both
the advice and Tom's suggestion for a more contemporary

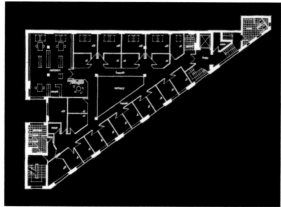

Opposite and below:
**Waltham Cross, 1981**
High-tech: J+W's colourful exercise
in providing workspace/storage in
Hertfordshire.

solution on the proviso that it should cost no more than the original design. Epsom and Ewell readily approved the significant change in appearance in just three weeks and the 'speculative' scheme was soon let to Sankey Building Supplies who also commissioned J+W for the low key fit out. "We didn't have much work on, so we detailed the building and finishes to death", says Jestico. "We questioned everything."

Waltham Cross was a similar story, the second project for the Epsom developer Trust Properties, who required a workspace/storage building that could be subdivided into four separate units, each with its own frontage, plus a mezzanine floor across one end. Truck roller shutters were used to provide access to incoming services, while the architects specified seamless glazing which was glued into place using car windscreen technology, thus avoiding the need for window frames. One of the key moves here was to solve a problem of tenants 'disfiguring' their buildings. So, the design allowed the resident companies to hang their signs on a red mesh grid panel, with air-conditioning units, burglar alarms and other paraphernalia behind. "The shop front, so to speak, was flexible and yet respectful of changing", says Whiles. The architects also concentrated all the services in one corner of the building, accessed through a roller shutter. But there were elements here that have stayed with the practice, such as using high quality ironmongery, or specifying larger, more generous doors, as well as working closely with contractors to get them on board and use their expertise too. "We try not to design money into foundations or drainage, where you can't see it", says Whiles. "We put our effort into design to where you touch—the handrail, the door handle, so that the feeling is of quality."

**1979** Conservative Government.
Margaret Thatcher Prime Minister

**1979** Sony Walkman
launched

**1979** J+W move to their
first office

30

PLUS
jestico + whiles

Waltham Cross, 1981
The long view: the scheme's red mesh
panels allowed a unified aesthetic, and
for tenants to hang their signage and
other paraphernalia behind.

So this was the age of technology, beyond the 'white heat' Harold Wilson and Tony Benn era when people were building high-tech factories and investing in industry. For J+W, whilst their industrial buildings had won awards and raised the practice's profile, work in the sector was a short-lived affair and the bulk of its workload would soon move on to offices and residential following this brief flirtation.

One such scheme with another colourful story attached to it was 55 Berkeley Square. This was a building bought by Texan oil and coal millionaire Stanley Seeger for himself and his personal assistant Penelope Midgley. Seeger had his apartment on the top two floors; offices were ranged on the bottom two, and Midgley had the floor in between. "He'd asked her to design the office of the future", recalls Whiles. On a recommendation, J+W found themselves designing this space, with everything about it leaning toward the high-tech and futuristic. The lighting had to come on as one walked into the room, the door had to 'melt' into the wall; glass partitions changed colour or went opaque at the flick of a switch to aid Seeger's reclusiveness. Everything was, as Whiles describes it, 'Bondish', even to the extent that a security expert was hired for his know-how in providing doors which slid open with a 'whoosh' as you approached them. In the end, Midgley resigned before completion, but J+W retained this particular 'bond'—going on to design a restaurant for her in Connaught Place.

Another scheme at the time had not dissimilar roots. A secretary at Farrell Grimshaw called Wendy Alexander had left to work for Henry Ford II, and J+W found itself working on Ford's swimming pool as a result. The scheme had suffered terrible condensation problems and needed re-roofing, so the architects gutted the pool and rebuilt the building.

Further conversions included two buildings for Friends of the Earth: the first on City Road, and the second in Underwood Street, nearby. The former was another scheme notable for the low budget on offer, but also importantly for the client's understandable enthusiasm for sustainable development principles. The existing listed building project included a solid fuel stove, recirculated air, fixed windows, low energy light fittings, and so on. Happily, Tom Jestico had always been interested in this low energy approach, ever since a visit to Australia prompted him and his then wife—an interior designer— to join the Intermediate Technology Group. This was all about products for the Third World—hand-driven pumps, windmills and the like. One of the group's membership was one Liz Kessler, the eventual client on the Friends of the Earth jobs. The Underwood Street scheme was a 1920s industrial building with fewer opportunities for more energy saving, so it became more of a fit-out job, with FoE as tenants here rather than owners, as they were with the City Road building.

Pedigree Petfoods,
Melton Mowbray, 1984
Fast food: J+W's work in Melton Mowbray
included an unrealised design for a truck
to help with the meat processing whose
innovation led to a further commission to
design offices.

Beginnings                                                          31

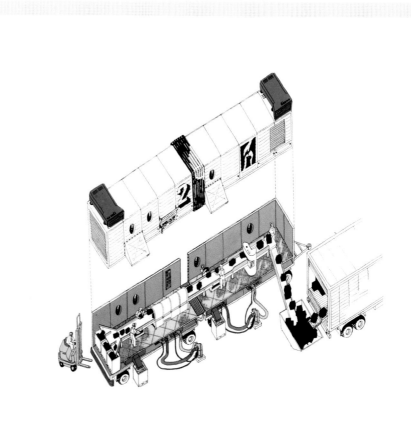

## Pedigree Petfoods

Pedigree Petfoods was an example of ingenuity in action. Having pulled off a familiar trick of appearing a bigger practice than they really were at the time, chiefly by imploring friends to populate the office during Pedigree's visit, Jestico + Whiles found themselves doing a number of projects for the firm. The company owned a meat stripping plant in Melton Mowbray, Leicestershire. Essentially this is where frozen meat—of all types—arrives on site and is then handled using a German tyre crusher machine, before the cooking and canning process. But the company was being thwarted from operating at night

because the site, which was problematically on a flood plain, also faced onto a residential area. It is a noisy business, meat. Rather than propose a new building, however, J+W put forward their idea for a 'styled-up' articulated container truck with crushers inside to sit at one end of the production line by day, and which could be taken to the far end, away from the residential area, at night. Planning permission would thus not be required. Although the scheme was never built, the firm admired this kind of innovative approach, and immediately asked J+W to design offices on the Melton Mowbray site instead. The resultant low-

cost scheme was largely a fit-out of an old industrial building, with windows punched into the wall.

Another job for the firm at the same site was for a canning cooling tower, the design for which had to go before Lord St John of Fawsley and Roy Strong at the Royal Fine Art Commission in St James's Square. As it was, this meeting was mostly concerned with the grey colour of the proposed tower. "Lord St John said: 'I think you're awfully nice chaps'", recalls Jestico. "And that was it." Approval was achieved, but the client elected for a design-build route.

was partially supported on it—something the firm never told the district surveyor. The client, though, was worried about vandalism, not just because of growing evidence of the phenomenon socially at the time but also because The Forum music venue had just opened nearby. "So we designed a chainmail curtain that went around the front on a track", says Whiles. "But it has never been put up, and nobody has ever touched it."

Competitions were never a big part of the practice's early years. But one did catch the attention. This was for a Munich swimming pool facility, the practice's first attempt to branch out overseas, well before it opened an office in Prague. The design again emphasised environmental efficiency, featuring scale-like solar collectors, a high degree of natural light and a nearby lake acting as a latent heat source. But it failed to make a splash in the contest. Did it put the firm off this way of getting work? Not particularly, but there was a practical lesson quite beyond a whetting of the appetite for Europe and its perceived higher quality standards and detailing. But competitions were perhaps too high risk. "If you were going to put your efforts anywhere", says Jestico, "there always seemed to be something to follow up which gave you a better chance of winning, other than by going into an unlimited competition, where you might be one of 1,000 entries. Somehow there was always a guy round the corner who, if

The backdrop to this quest for low-energy schemes, of course, was the oil crisis, rather than anything to do with climate change. But looking back, the strands of these separate worlds of clients—Whiles' individual developer-led clients and Jestico's clients with a more institutional thrust—were complementary, and unquestioned at the time.

Another small scheme in the early days, around 1986, involved the estate agent McHugh & Co., which fronted a Grade II listed Georgian house in Kentish Town. Chris McHugh was an advisor to and close personal friend of developer/contractor Peter Fitzpatrick for whom J+W were designing their innovative mixed-use housing and light industrial scheme at Bruges Place, following their recommendation by Sam Price of Structural Engineers Price & Myers. McHugh's site was on a prominent position at the top of Kentish Town Road where the practice created a striking green glass facade for the scheme, with materials brought in from Canada, and with a roof which

Munich Swimming Pool competition, 1988
Talent pool: this rare competition entry
concentrated on environmental efficiency,
natural light and scale-like solar collectors.

Beginnings

33

you just phoned him up, you might be one of three or one of four. The odds seemed to be better for picking up work."

The flavour of these early years, then, was clear. They were a time of experimentation, of moving offices, gaining experience, creating 'silk purses from sow's ears', of attaining maximum value for clients and forging a belief that a site could be transformed from inauspicious beginnings. For Whiles it was also about suddenly meeting a broad range of clients—from private individuals building their houses, to Mars, one of the biggest companies in the world. Or from the Policy Studies Institute to the Royal Fine Arts Commission. "Every day was a delight because you woke up in the morning not knowing really who you were going to meet", said Whiles. "That's what I thought was very rich about architecture. It was just terrific, the whole range, and it made you think on your feet and modify your behaviour, even down to the right coloured ties for different boroughs."

But another experience from those early years perhaps goes to the heart of the practice's ethos. The firm undertook some Myers-Briggs psychometric testing at the RIBA. This, though, flummoxed the testers, principally because, having been doing such experiments for some ten years across the world, they had never yet been presented with such diametrically opposing indications and answers to what were essentially the same questions. Whiles finishes the story: "We frowned, and looked at them, and said: 'well, that's the only way we can do architecture. We have to be different things, to different people, at different times.'"

**Below and opposite:**
Machines for working in: Influenced by
Team Four's Reliance Controls electronics
factory in Swindon, this warehouse was
one of J+W's early forays into industrial
architecture on a low budget.

# Case Study:
# Epsom, 1981

Beyond the conversions that were the lifeblood of the firm's early years, Jestico + Whiles was also designing contemporary new buildings. Honoured with an Industrial Architecture Award by *The Financial Times*, and reviewed favourably by Deyan Sudjic, then of *Building Design*, the Epsom warehouse on the Longmead Industrial Estate was the first of a series of 'sheds' for a nationwide industrial developer, constructed in a simple, economic portal frame. A raised parapet lent the structure greater elegance, while basic repetitive casements, bolted together on a purpose-made support, helped to create a strong

identity and bright interior on what was a low budget. The 2,000 square metre scheme also features reversed Crittall windows, used primarily because they were a cost-effective solution, with a requested pitched roof of five degrees which was hipped at both ends, thus giving the impression of a flat roof. Built during a period where many speculative office developments were being encouraged, the building also featured a studded rubber floor and an early use of intumescent paint. Jestico recalls how the key influences, certainly in terms of looking as though it had a flat roof and vertical silver cladding,

included Team Four's 1967 Reliance Controls electronics factory in Swindon, that practice's final 'hurrah'. But there are also distinct echoes of the bright green framing James Stirling had just used to good effect on the Neue Staatsgalerie in Stuttgart, Germany. Finally, one other particular cost-saving feature of the building had an interesting lineage—a member of the building team steadfastly refused to put any steel reinforcement in the concrete floor, having laid many miles of runway for airstrips this way during the war. If it could take an aeroplane landing on it without the extra, it could take anything.

Interventions

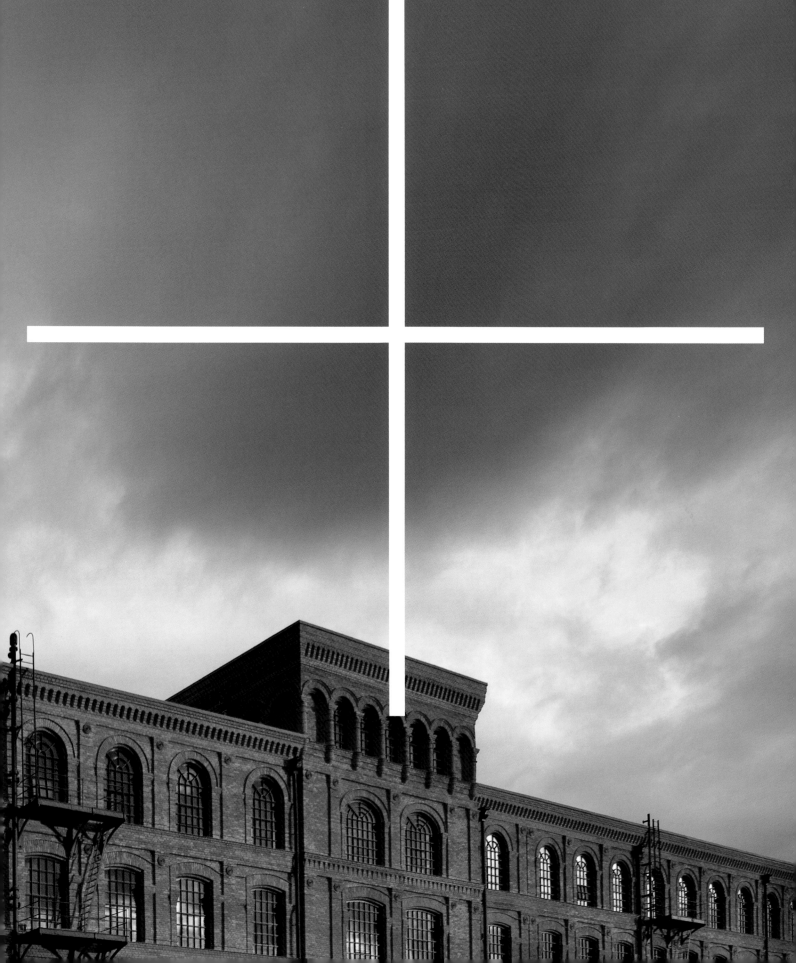

British Council, Prague, 1991–1992
A spectacular early-Modern ceiling has been
restored as the centrepiece of the British
Council's new centre in Prague. Glass blocks
cast into the floor transmit daylight even
deeper down to the basement.

# Interventions

On 9 November 1989, the Berlin Wall came tumbling
down, along with the entire Soviet empire of Central and
Eastern Europe. Jestico + Whiles quickly became caught
up in this ferment of liberation. By early 1992 the practice
had set up the first foreign architect's office in Prague
and, later the same year, their first building in the city was
opened by former political prisoner and then Czechoslovak
President, Vaclav Havel.

En route, the practice also picked up marketable expertise
in another sector of architectural design: interventions in,
and conservation of, historic buildings. And, as is evident
in the ten buildings featured in this chapter, the practice
has contributed several ingenious design concepts to
this genre that were ahead of their time. These design
concepts can be traced back to the practice's roots in
small extensions and conversions in England and to its
technical, quasi-engineering approach. Natural daylighting,
passive ventilation and heat retention in the building fabric
are all recurrent themes that lower the buildings' energy
consumption and carbon footprints. As for their style,
director Heinz Richardson says: "These interventions are all
unashamedly contemporary, very calm and modern. They
enhance the historic architecture rather than reproduce or
ape or disguise it."

So when liberation came to half of Europe in late 1989, had
J+W been waiting all along to join in with their drawing

boards cocked and at the ready? Well, not exactly. "It was a
case of mistaken identity", recalls Tom Jestico. "In 1991, we
were asked by a friend of a friend of mine to visit Budapest
and assess the market viability of the government's large,
architectural department there. This visit was picked up in
the British press by the British Council. They thought we had
established our own Hungarian office and asked us to design
a new centre there."

The practice lost the bid for the Budapest centre, but it won
another British Council centre in Prague. The Prague centre
was to be converted out of a classic of those early Modernist
buildings of the 1920s for which Czechoslovakia was famed.
Its great central hall was drenched in daylight streaming
down through a spectacular racetrack-shaped glass ceiling
directly below a fully-glazed roof. The hall emitted clear
echoes of Otto Wagner's astonishing Post Office Savings
Bank of 1911 in Vienna. Robert Collingwood of J+W
continued the homage to Wagner by casting glass blocks in
the floor that, just as in its Viennese precursor, transmitted
daylight further down into the basement, which would now
serve as a library. For good measure, Collingwood added a
glass desk over a central hole in the floor that doubled as a
lightwell for the library below.

When it came to building the conversion, Collingwood
recoiled from the 'chaos' he had encountered at the British
embassy site in Prague, where British workmen were

**1989** Unemployment at its
lowest for ten years

**1989** Mrs Thatcher celebrates
ten years in power

**1989** House of Commons
televised

employed by a British contractor. Instead he persuaded his client to use local skills and materials, challenging the convictions of many Czechs and most foreigners that local materials were shoddy and local skills non-existent. "I argued that, as skilled tradesmen were only paid £50 a month, they could do the work again and again within the budget", he recalls. "In fact, with the help of local architect Surpmo, the work was finished beautifully first time,

before the deadline and below budget." The crowning moment came when the centre was opened by President Vaclav Havel, who celebrated this trail-blazing collaboration between British and Czech firms.

Halfway through the Prague project came another British Council centre: this one in Madrid. It was to be converted out of a fine Palladian villa, which had been listed, making any

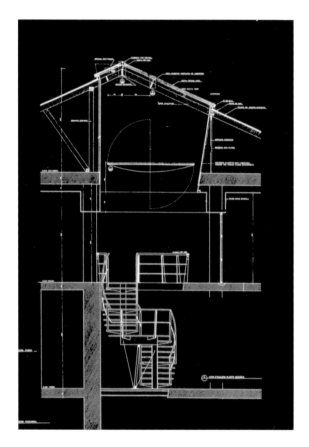

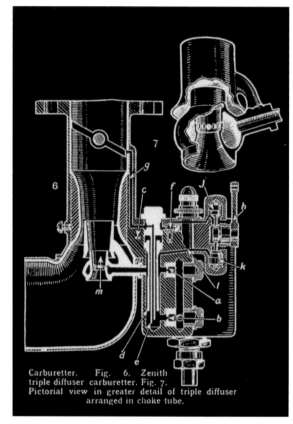

Carburetter. Fig. 6. Zenith
triple diffuser carburetter. Fig. 7.
Pictorial view in greater detail of triple diffuser
arranged in choke tube.

external alterations or extensions taboo. So, continuing along
the same route started in Prague, J+W smuggled daylight
surreptitiously deep into the heart of the building. They did
more than that. They came up with an ingenious device that
was inspired by a petrol engine carburettor and controls not
only daylighting but also natural ventilation and cooling.

Natural daylighting and ventilation starts at the crest of
the roof, which was partly replaced with a glazed vent that
precisely matched the existing roofline. Directly underneath,
elliptical slots were punched through a ceiling and the floor
below to funnel daylight down—and through—a newly
inserted lightweight staircase with perforated steel steps.
From the foot of the staircase, daylight was transmitted
even deeper down two more storeys through steel mesh
inserted in the floors. In total, a cone of daylight was
punched right through the building from roof right down
to basement.

The really clever device is a yellow fabric flap installed in
the loft. The flap rotates just like the butterfly valve in a
carburettor, as envisaged by J+W's Tony Ingram, to control
the flow of both daylight and air. On bright, hot summer
days, the translucent flap is shut to filter the sunshine and
to contain the air above as it heats up before escaping
through high-level roof vents. On bright, cool winter
days, the flap is also shut, but this time the warmed air is
channelled off into public rooms via a fan-assisted duct.

In a slightly later project in Prague, a building with Medieval
vaults in the city centre was converted to offices. Here a
modern glazed ambulatory was inserted into the central
courtyard that gave under-cover access to all ground floor
rooms yet left the historic fabric structurally and visually intact.

Closer to home, very similar passive environmental
controls were applied to an office conversion in London's

Opposite:
**Ericsson Palace, Prague, 1994–1996**
A new glazed ambulatory gives under-
cover access to all ground floor rooms of
Ericsson Palace in Prague city centre. The
listed historic building has been left intact.

## First foreign architect's office in Prague

In 1992, a few months into the British Council centre project in Prague, Jestico + Whiles director Robert Collingwood set up the first UK architect's office in Czechoslovakia since the fall of Communism. A few months later, he had had enough of commuting back and forth from London, so with his wife and two small children he moved out to Prague. The office he established has remained J+W's only office outside London ever since.

A year later, after the British Council centre in Prague was officially opened by Czech President Vaclav Havel, "the phone never stopped ringing", he recalls. This was during Czechoslovakia's Velvet Revolution when clients, most of them Western, were falling over each other to get projects built. "I had also become a local hero", he adds, "because I had trusted Czechs to design and build the centre."

Picking up commissions and staffing the office, mainly with locals, was therefore no big struggle. Staff grew to 25 in number, and remained at that level until the current Europe-wide recession slashed that number by half.

In 2001, Sean Clifton took over the Prague office after Collingwood returned to England to set up on his own. "We now have retail, residential and hotel projects all over the world, sometimes working closely with the London office", says Clifton. "We've also won competitions to masterplan whole new towns of 50,000 people in Omsk and Moscow."

1992 'Cones hotline' introduced

Stukeley Street, London, 1992–1994
The dingy old lightwell in London's Covent
Garden has been converted into a smart
glass-roofed atrium. This now brightens
up the gloomy interiors of a former
warehouse and flushes them with fresh
air by the natural stack effect.

Covent Garden in 1992–1994. As Heinz Richardson recollects, this was a sustainable approach without energy-guzzling air-conditioning that was stimulated by the third oil crisis of 1990, when Iraq's invasion of Kuwait doubled the price of oil, and it was conceived without the aid of an environmental engineer.

The existing building on Stukeley Street was a six-storey late Victorian warehouse with deep, gloomy interiors that drew little relief from a dank narrow lightwell. J+W then set to work transforming the lightwell by removing 24 old sash windows opening on to it. These were replaced with clear-glazed sliding doors that stretched from floor to ceiling. Next, the lightwell was capped in an S-shaped glazed roof incorporating perforated stainless steel sheets that reflect low sunlight while allowing daylight and air to pass through. Then, glass lifts, with glazed access bridges that block as little daylight as possible, were inserted into the lightwell.

Finally, the sliding doors were linked to a smoke detector that activates their closure in the event of a fire.

Throughout the year, the large glazed doors channel daylight into the heart of the building. In winter, the lightwell warms up to a pleasant 16°C in the reflected sunshine with the roof vents shut. In summer, sunlight and the prevailing wind work in harness to flush cool fresh air by the stack effect through the offices and up through the open roof vents. In this way, the lightwell acts as a lung through which the whole building breathes naturally, according to the designer Tony Ingram.

Over in St James's Square, a more elongated old lightwell was tackled in similar fashion in 1993–1996 for the recording company PolyGram. The lightwell was transformed into a naturally ventilated atrium by capping it with a glass roof, while a narrow footbridge links company departments at

**PolyGram, London, 1993–1996**
An elongated old lightwell in London's
St James's Square was capped over
and brightened up for PolyGram. A new
footbridge now links departments at
opposite ends, while a staff cafe relaxes
down below.

PolyGram, London, 1993–1994
Sliding glass partitions fulfil the recording
company's desire for avant-garde style
and flexibility.

Opposite: Independiente Drill Hall,
London, 1996–1997
Chic and sumptuous modern offices
luxuriate inside the old timber and brick
shell of a former drill hall in Chiswick.

Independiente Drill Hall, London,
1996–1997
Two overtly modern office floors were shoe-
horned into the former drill hall without
scarring its curved timber arches. Glazed
partitions and floors channel daylight from
rooflights down to the ground floor.

opposite ends without disturbing departments in between.
Below that, a cafe warmed by underfloor heating revels in
ample daylight and headroom.

The next client was Independiente, an independent record
label distributed by PolyGram. Here two floors of offices
were shoe-horned into a deep-plan Arts and Crafts drill hall
in Chiswick while letting its distinctive timber arches and
beams still shine through. Once again, plenty of glass was
used in partitions and floors to let daylight penetrate from
rooflights down to the ground floor.

Then, in 1997, J+W bought a building near Euston Station
and converted it into its own offices. It had been built in
1834 before the railway era as a two-storey stable block
for horses serving a long-vanished canal basin. 15 years
after the conversion, here is a practice, with a track record
in modern industrial buildings, that is clearly very much at

home in this industrial building of an earlier era, with its
stock-brick walls, exposed jack-arch floors and cast-iron
columns and beams. The practice has even added one of
its trademark industrial building components: a Crawford
up-and-over door that is opened up on warm summer days
to let fresh air and daylight gush in. The purchase and
conversion of the building was entirely paid for by raising
the original timber roof by two metres, inserting seven
new flats and selling them off.

Another industrial conversion carried out in 2005 demonstrates
the practice's breezy, non-deferential approach to old industrial
buildings. At Worship Street in London's East End, a charitable
trust developer wanted to give a facelift to utilitarian early
twentieth century warehouses and let them out to creative
industry firms. J+W responded by completely rebuilding
the shared entrance, reception and service core in an eye-
catchingly flash, modern style with a facade of translucent,

**Cobourg Street, London, 1997–1998**
Being steeped in contemporary industrial
architecture, J+W have found their natural
home in a canal building of 1834 vintage.
They have added a modern up-and-over
industrial door and a top floor of flats for sale.

1996 Unemployment falls
below two million

Below and opposite:
Worship Street, London, 2005
In converting old workshops tucked down
a narrow mews in London's East End, the
reception and services core was totally
rebuilt in eye-catchingly jazzy style.

insulated Kalwall. They upgraded the office units themselves
in an updated utility style with, instead of ceilings, an exposed,
though carefully coordinated, array of pipes, cables and ceiling
heating ducts that exhale warm air uniformly through vivid
orange fabric jackets.

At the other extreme, J+W has also taken architectural
conservation to its purest restoration limits. At the Foundling
Museum in Bloomsbury, three grand Grade I listed rooms
of 1745, including one with an amazingly ornate Rococo
ceiling, were painstakingly restored in 2007. Ceilings on the
verge of collapse were secured, decorations were reinstated
to match the originals after exhaustive investigations, as
shown on pages 54 and 55, and up-to-date environmental
controls were installed with all modern pipes, wires and
sensors fully concealed. Yet alongside these three restored
historic rooms, the practice designed several overtly modern
galleries. What made this incongruous combination of

architectural styles acceptable to English Heritage was that
the museum building itself was different again: it was built
in 1938 in the Neo-Georgian style.

The largest intervention tackled by J+W is at a huge
derelict cotton factory in the Manchester of Poland, Łódź.
In 2008 it was converted into a flash new hotel. It can be
viewed as the practice's own office conversion in Cobourg
Street writ large. It is also far more ambitious and exciting,
as can be seen in the Case Study on page 56–63.

1997  Diana killed in car crash

Worship Street, London, 2005
The new reception and services core was
designed with as much care and attention
as a self-contained new building.

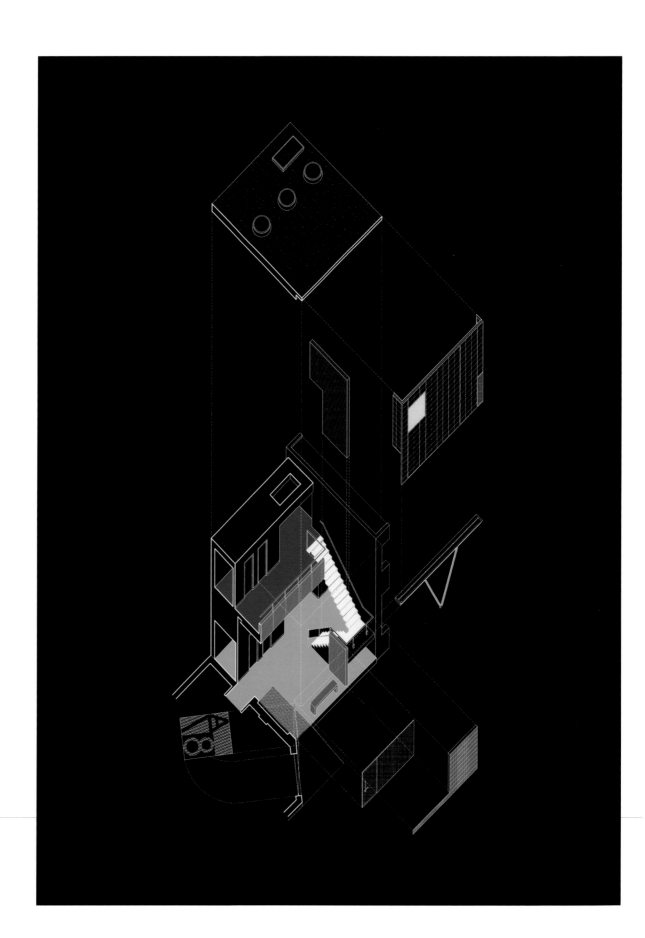

**Worship Street, London, 2005**
The interiors of the early twentieth
century utilitarian workshops were
upgraded in twenty-first century
utilitarian manner.

Interventions

53

Foundling Museum, London, 2004–2007
The Museum's Neo-Georgian building of
1938 vintage was discreetly enlarged with
a modest modern extension at the rear.

1998
BMW acquires Rolls Royce Motors

Foundling Museum, London, 2004–2007
A modern gallery and a faithfully restored
classical gallery of 1745 coexist happily within
the Neo-Georgian Museum building.

1999 First elected assemblies in
Scotland and Wales

1999 Ernie Wise dies

# Case Study:
# Andel's Hotel, Łódź,
# 2009

How do you convert an enormous, grim, rectangular nineteenth century factory into a fun twenty-first century hotel? Simple: you line both long external walls with bedrooms and open up the cavernous interior as a toplit atrium. Job done.

Except that the old factory acquired by the Austrian-owned Andel's 'design hotel' chain had been one of Europe's largest textile mills. It was a grand, classical palace of a building erected in 1852 in Łódź. All 180 guestrooms and 80 long-stay apartments could be happily installed each behind its own large factory window, while leaving the ornate exterior virtually intact.

But the sticking point came with the atrium. The building's five immense floors were so lofty and wide that a plain vanilla central atrium would be disappointingly featureless and empty.

So Jestico + Whiles' interior designers came up with a 'tutti-frutti' alternative that would be far more lip-smacking. In the design by J+W's interiors group and executive architect OP Architekten, three cone-shaped holes, or 'light cones', were punched at raking angles along the centreline of the building and down through its full height. The holes left in each floor are not quite elliptical in shape and lined in smooth

Opposite and below:
Dazzling multicoloured displays are regularly
staged by the three light cones, thanks to
advanced LED lighting.

**Opposite:**
Textiles manufactured in the original
factory were researched and recreated
throughout the new hotel.

Interventions
Case Study

61

**Below:**
A rooftop swimming pool was converted
out of a fire-fighting water tank directly
above the wellness centre.

**Below:**
The restaurant layout echoes the
original grid of cast-iron columns
and beams and brick jack arches.

**Opposite:**
The elongated seven-storey shell of
the nineteenth century factory neatly
accommodates 260 bedrooms and
apartments plus the social facilities of
a twenty-first century hotel.

balustrading. During the day, the light cones project wide shafts of daylight deep into the heart of the building. At night, the balustrades transform into kinetic sculptures, when LED lights wash them in shifting sequences of vivid colours, and occasionally when films are projected to create weird, distorted, abstract cinema.

The factory's original grid of cast iron columns was left exposed in the wide circulation spaces between rows of guestrooms, as well as in the vast reception hall on the ground floor and in the rooftop restaurant, bar and lounge room. So too were the original brick jack-arch floors and brick walls, down to the roughly patched repairs carried out in later decades. Huge relics of heavy machinery were displayed to sculptural effect.

An exciting counterpoint is set up between the funky, irregular, brightly coloured and skittish new insertions and the craggy, regimented, massive and rigid old fabric. A journey was created where, as J+W intended, guests happen upon everything and delight in the surprises.

The hotel's *piece de resistance* is the new swimming pool. It is perched right on top of the building with a sun terrace and glazed viewing gallery that cantilevers precariously over the front facade. The swimming pool actually occupies a huge water tank that fed the factory's sprinkler system. The cast-iron tank was cut up, removed, sand-blasted, reinstated and then lined with stainless steel. Not something an architect or interior designer would attempt in the UK.

The conversion was completed in 2009. With the design concept developed here, Andel was able to market the hotel at four stars rather than three stars.

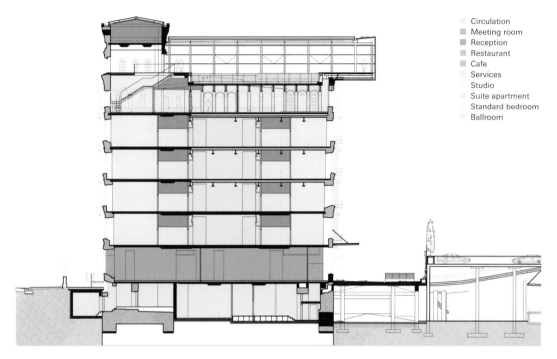

Circulation
Meeting room
Reception
Restaurant
Cafe
Services
Studio
Suite apartment
Standard bedroom
Ballroom

SECTION

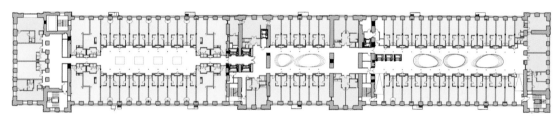

UPPER FLOOR PLAN

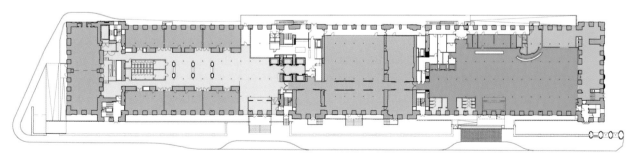

GROUND FLOOR PLAN

Living

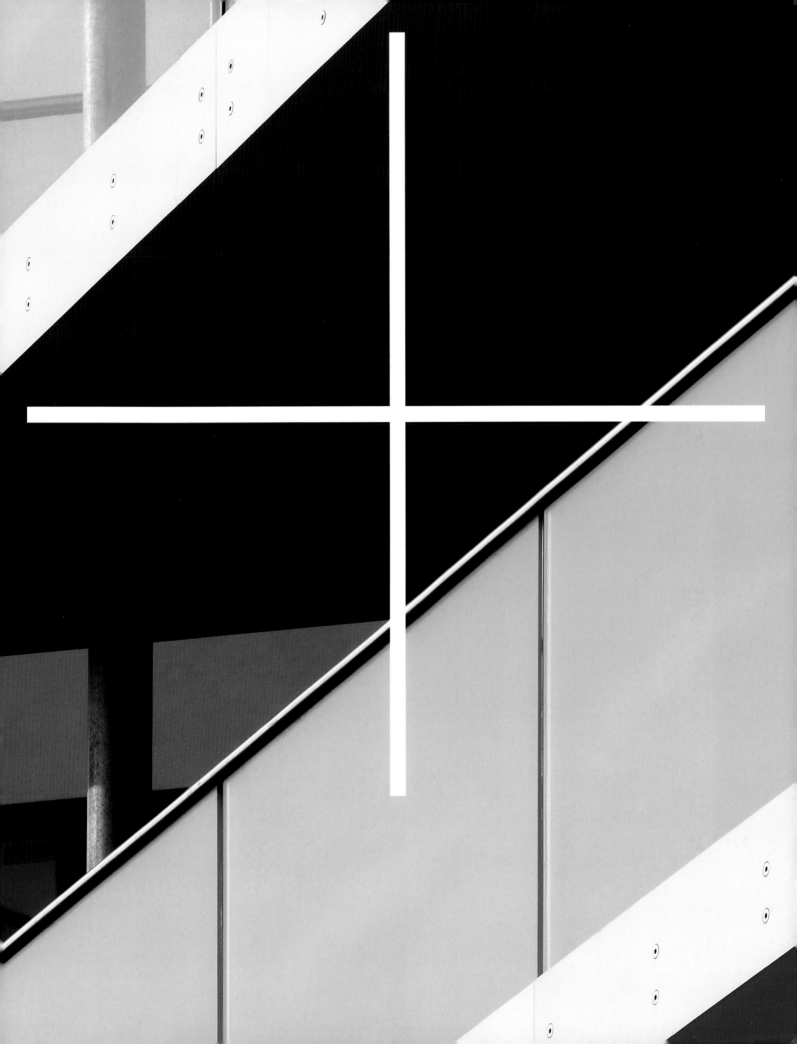

Bruges Place, London, 1984–1986
Living over the shop was reinvented
with this revolutionary pairing of two-
storey maisonettes above two-storey
business units.

# Living

Jestico + Whiles' first introduction into new-build housing
came in 1984 through the standard, time-honoured route of
local networking. The practice was approached by developer/
contractor Peter Fitzpatrick on the recommendation of a
mutual friend, Sam Price, of structural engineer Price &
Myers, both firms of north London. Fitzpatrick had acquired
a site at Bruges Place in Kentish Town that came with a
standard problem. Fitzpatrick wanted to develop it as housing
for sale, whereas Camden Council had zoned it as industrial.

"We told Fitzpatrick that we didn't see this as a problem",
recollects John Whiles. So, instead of either housing
or industry, he proposed both housing and industry. A
four-storey scheme was built in which two storeys of
maisonettes were neatly stacked on top of two storeys of
B1 business units. Both maisonettes and business units
were arranged in two parallel rows on either side of central
walkways that give access on the ground floor and second
floor. The first floor oversails car parking at ground level
and provides generous terraces for the maisonettes above.
This first foray into housing won two key accolades: an
RIBA award and a Housing Design Award. The scheme also
reinstated the common arrangement before the advent of
land-use planning of living above the shop. It was indeed
hailed as launching a new building type—live-work units—
though, in Bruges Place, there are no internal connections
between homes and workplaces.

In the 1980s, Docklands in run-down east London exploded
into a developers' klondyke. Development fever was
stoked up by Margaret Thatcher's environment secretary,
Michael Heseltine when, in 1981 he set up a Development
Corporation for the area and an Enterprise Zone, effectively
a planning free-for-all area, on the Isle of Dogs. J+W was
invited to join the 'Eastenders' bonanza by developer Keith
Preston of Kentish Homes.

In 1987, the practice won a design competition staged by
Preston for Burrell's Wharf in the Isle of Dogs, the Grade II
listed former shipyard where IK Brunel built the legendary
*Great Eastern*, the largest ship in the world, in 1858. As
John Whiles recollects, "Preston had a vision for a lifestyle
and a scheme that would generate a new neighbourhood
around it." Preston's intended lifestyle was not aimed at
conventional families with children but at yuppies cashing
in on the privatisation of City stock markets.

Fresh from visiting industrial areas in Paris, Whiles
responded to Preston's vision by playing up the raw,
industrial nature of the site and adding a dash of continental
lifestyle. The former shipyard now comprises a series of
calm, traffic-free courtyards, achieved by sinking 350 car
parking spaces below the largest courtyard. Some 365
homes were created at a deceptively high density of 500
bedspaces per hectare.

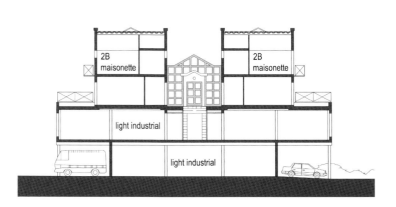

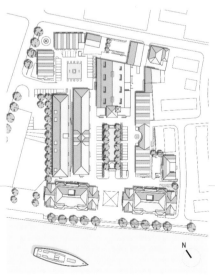

**1990** BREEAM standards
introduced

Opposite and below:
Burrell's Wharf, London, 1987–1995
IK Brunel's shipyard was converted
into 365 homes enclosing landscaped
courtyards and two giant new-build
villas on the riverfront. A fitness centre,
community hall and business units are
also included.

Living                                                           69

Burrell's Wharf culminates in two new-build, nine-storey apartment blocks that stand like imposing, apartment blocks modelled on traditional dock warehouses on the riverfront. Treatment is rugged in keeping with the converted industrial buildings yet updated without pastiche by using large precast concrete panels and steel windows. The new community's heart now throbs in a large central building which once was the scene of huge iron plates being shaped to clad the *Great*

*Eastern* but now contains business units, community hall and fitness centre with swimming pool.

Burrell's Wharf was not completed until 1994, seven years after the design competition. During construction, the project was badly hit, and very nearly killed off, by Black Monday, the infamous stock market crash of 19 October 1987. The project (not the developer) was jettisoned into receivership, and in the process nearly the entire team of developer, contractor and consultants was sacked. The sole exception was J+W, which was deemed to be central to the design concept. The plug was pulled on Burrell's Wharf by the Halifax Building Society in a fit of anxiety over its first loan to a commercial housebuilder. "They appointed a noted receiver, Tony Richmond of KPMG", adds John Whiles. "Some years later he claimed that this single act at Burrell's Wharf set off the whole property recession that lasted well into the 90s."

J+W's first involvement with public-sector housing came in 1991, when it won a design competition sponsored by a community housing association. This was Camden Gardens, back on the firm's home turf of north London.

The completed scheme is an elegant, symmetrical composition of three villa blocks along the public street in front and an elongated block overlooking the Regent's Canal at the back. All four blocks are similar in scale, form and facing brickwork to the surrounding Victorian townscape.

Below and opposite:
Camden Gardens, London, 1991–1993
J+W's first social housing scheme is
elegantly arranged as three villa blocks
and one terrace enclosing traffic-free
courtyards.

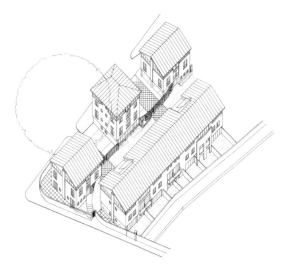

Without any sign of strain, the scheme packs in some 27
affordable apartments, maisonettes and houses at a higher
density than Camden's planners had stipulated. And arguing
that not all affordable housing residents have cars, J+W cut
car parking provision from 100 per cent to just 60 per cent
of dwellings, leaving the centre of the site free and secure
as a communal playspace.

Then in 1997, it was back to the Isle of Dogs and more
private housing. An Essex housebuilder, Furlong Homes, had
bought a prize riverfront site at Ocean Wharf, and the London
Docklands Development Corporation (LDDC) recommended
six architects that might improve on the planning permission
that came with the site.

"Our name happened to be at the top of the list, and Jim
Furlong and another director came round to see us on a
Friday", recalls Heinz Richardson. "We bashed out a scheme

72

PLUS
jestico + whiles

Ocean Wharf, London, 1997–1999
An elliptical 12-storey tower salutes the
river in marine style with curved balconies,
while a lower oblong block lies alongside.

for them by Monday, and they were so thrilled with it they appointed us without seeing the others on the list."

J+W's thrilling scheme at Ocean Wharf salutes the river with a sleek, elliptical tower 12 storeys high. Alongside it, a seven-storey slab block runs at right angles to the river, though it gives all occupants oblique views of the river across an adjoining park. Curved balconies overlooking the river are critical ingredients of the tower's classy elliptical shape, and Heinz Richardson is particularly pleased that Furlong adopted J+W's expensive curved glass balustrading rather than cheap metal railings. "This helped to set Furlong in a different league", he adds.

Four years later, in 2001, J+W ventured even further into east London by winning a competition for Furlong Homes that tackles a large, desolate site at the most remote end of the Royal Docks. Royal Quay was built as a high-density

development of 440 homes with three elliptical towers, like Ocean Wharf in triplicate, to give it sparkle. As an extra twist, these three towers appear to float directly over the water. The quayside around the towers was submerged just half a metre below water level, a clever ploy that also made intrusive safety railings dispensable and brings people closer to the water.

Royal Quay's other special attraction is a late Victorian hotel, where passengers including Charles Dickens stayed before embarking by ship across the world. This ornate Arts and Crafts building has now been converted to a combined business centre, fitness centre and cafe-restaurant that forms the centrepiece of the masterplan and focus of the community.

Three years earlier in 1998, the practice won an open design competition for the House for the Future, in Wales, that attracted 49 entries. Overnight, this competition win established the practice in the premier league of sustainable

A trio of marine-style elliptical towers
rises out of the water in the Royal Docks.
Behind them stand rectilinear blocks and
a converted Arts and Crafts hotel.

design architects. "We followed up sustainable ideas from this scheme and used them in later schemes and competition entries", says Heinz Richardson. "We also set up a Green Team in the practice on the strength of it." (See Case Study on pages 78–79.)

The practice's first elderly housing project came about largely because of, not in spite of, its lack of experience in this

field. "We'd been working with the Peabody Trust on and off", relates John Whiles. "Then in 1999 the development director, Dickon Robinson, asked us to come up with a new, enlightened approach for housing old people on a site at Darwin Court near the Elephant and Castle."

"We studied schemes in Holland and Sweden, and the more we looked into it the more we wanted Darwin Court

Below and opposite:
**Darwin Court, London, 1999-2001**
So sociable and welcoming is this mould-breaking accommodation for ageing people that residents' offspring like to visit them rather than *vice-versa*. A lounge, dining hall and circulation route all merge together on the ground floor.

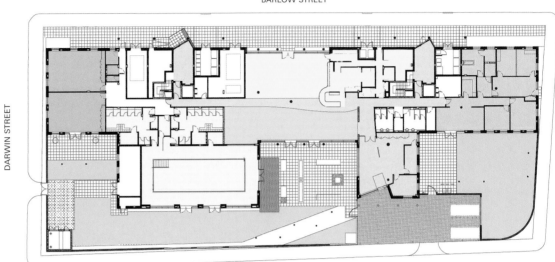

BARLOW STREET

DARWIN STREET

CATESBY STREET

CRAIL ROW

N

GROUND FLOOR PLAN
▢ Entrances and circulation
▢ Cafe and kitchen
▢ Lounge
▢ Pool and change
▢ Health care suite/administration
▢ Community space
▢ Lawn

to be community-focused", continues Whiles. "And the existing residents asked for their new homes to be so attractive that their relatives would want to visit them, not the other way round."

This inclusive approach struck a chord not only with Dickon Robinson but also with Southwark Council, which contributed some funding. The end result was a six-storey block containing 76 apartments and frail elderly care facilities. Its innovative, inclusive facilities are a health centre, skills-training centre, cafe-restaurant and fitness centre complete with swimming pool, all of which are open to local residents.

Darwin Court's attractive, inclusive, communal character is amply expressed in its architecture. Both lift lobbies on each floor lie next to south-facing terraces where residents can sun themselves and take tea with their neighbours. And on the ground floor, the reception desk, cafe-restaurant, lounge

and main circulation route are all open plan. "It's all very Scandinavian and what the hotel business calls 'the lobby culture'", comments John Whiles. "Everyone likes to sit in the front hall and see people coming and going."

Darwin Court was held up as one of just two UK model exemplars by the government-sponsored Housing our Ageing Population: Panel for Innovation, or HAPPI, in 2009. The scheme's acclaimed success at integrating older people into the wider community also opened doors for J+W into the healthcare sector. Pioneering projects include two residential care centres for older people in Margate and Tenterden, where Kent County Council and East Kent NHS joined forces to bring together social and health services.

Yet another Docklands project with Jim Furlong came along in 2002, though by now he had set up a new company, Telford Homes. This project at Abbotts Wharf blossomed

Below and opposite:
Parkville Apartments, Bratislava,
2007–2008
These luxury apartment blocks are set in
greenery in remembrance of a vineyard
they replace, while all cars are banished
underground.

into something much richer than private housing for sale. It
was a mixed-tenure scheme owned and developed in a true
partnering joint venture with East Thames Housing Group, as
featured on pages 80–81.

A few hundred miles further east, the practice's Prague
office picked up a luxury residential development for Orco,
a Czech-French developer for which it had previously
designed a couple of hotels. Completed in 2008, the
scheme named Parkville Apartments makes the most of
what had been a vineyard on a hill overlooking the capital of
Slovakia, Bratislava. Ten pavilions were carefully positioned
across the site and angled so as to give 90 per cent of
the 87 apartments spectacular views across the city to its
castle. Then the car parking was hidden underground so
that the site remains draped in greenery, including green
roofs covering all the pavilions.

The glamorous apartments sold for the highest price per
square metre ever paid for private housing in Slovakia.
It then went on to scoop the country's award for best
residential development.

Housing is only one of J+W's large array of design skills. Yet
as its many Housing Design Awards from 1989 onwards
testify, the practice has consistently held its own against
architects specialising in housing. And, as this chapter
shows, the practice consistently delivers homes with kerb
appeal—whatever tenure mix, density, technical innovations
or construction cost the client may demand.

**Left:**
The sustainable showhouse's living
spaces absorb ample daylight through
south-facing glazing.

**Right:**
Houses can easily be joined up into
a terrace.

# Case Study:
# House for the Future,
# Cardiff, 1998–2000

The House for the Future is arguably the UK's only permanent showhouse of sustainable architecture. It was built in 2000 alongside the historic buildings of the National Museum of Wales at St Fagans outside Cardiff to mark the new millennium by portraying a vision of the future. The brief was for a family house that would be carbon-neutral and could be built on a modest budget of £120,000.

The design by Jestico + Whiles and ECD Energy & Environment was selected through an open design competition that attracted 49 entries. It pioneered many green, sustainable features that have since become commonplace. Passive energy-saving features include large south-facing windows to admit solar energy, massive ground floor and internal walls to dampen temperature swings, a stack vent next to the central roof ridge and high thermal insulation. On the active side, they include solar water heaters, photovoltaic cells, ground-source heat pump and a wood-pellet heater.

The two practices added their own stipulation that, wherever possible, materials should be sourced within 50 miles of the site. The intention was not only to reduce embodied energy arising from transport but also to encourage jobs in the area. Consequently, Welsh oak was used for both the structural frame and external cladding. Riven Welsh slate was laid on the ground floor slab and recycled slates on the roof. And lime for render was manufactured in Brecon. Other local natural materials arrived by more fascinating routes. An internal partition that doubles as a heat sink was built out of blocks made with clay dug from the building site itself. The clay was compressed into blocks using a hand-operated ram and cured on site but, since the partition would be protected from the elements, there was no need to fire the blocks.

Local sheep's wool was used for thermal insulation. It had to be washed, treated against fire and insects, and then made into

**Right:**
The sustainable house harnesses
sunlight, wind and rain.

**Below:**
Recycled Welsh slates are combined
with high-tech solar collectors and
photovoltaic cells.

Living
Case Study

79

stiff batts by weaving in latex fibre. But as no factory in Wales was capable of performing these operations, the wool had to be sent to Germany and back—in one stroke cancelling out the project's local sourcing imperative.

J+W went as far as designing a modular system for the house. This opened up a multitude of configurations which spec housebuilders could use to satisfy any number of household requirements and site geometries. Even so, no housebuilders, not even the showhouse contractor, Redrow, have taken the opportunity of rolling out the house and its permutations across any of

their development sites. Heinz Richardson comments darkly: "What we learnt was that most housebuilders were incapable of even understanding the issues of sustainability, never mind building it."

As for J+W, it needed no persuading to join in the Welsh sustainability-fest. It absorbed all the latest theory and technical expertise of sustainable architecture. And it basked in all the free publicity. "The BBC broadcast three half-hour TV programmes about it", purrs Heinz Richardson. "And the showhouse had over two million visitors, virtually as many as visited the Millennium Dome."

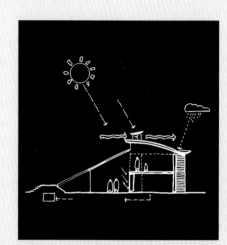

Top:
Two oblong apartment blocks overlook a
newly-created canal basin.

Bottom:
Sharp glazed balconies counterpoint flat
render facades.

Opposite:
A tower block rises on one side of the
apartment blocks.

# Case Study:
# Abbotts Wharf,
# London, 2002–2006

"Abbotts Wharf does a lot of things that capture the spirit of the age", says Heinz Richardson. It also fulfils key policies of the London Plan drawn up by the then Mayor, Ken Livingstone. Completed in 2006, the scheme regenerated a disused industrial site in Limehouse, on the northern fringes of Docklands, as housing. It put the site to intense use by packing in 201 dwellings at the eye-wateringly high density of 885 habitable rooms per hectare, partly by reducing car parking to just 0.43 spaces per dwelling. And it combined private and affordable housing on an equal 50/50 split for the first time.

Jestico + Whiles' solution answers this unusually tough brief and sets an inspired new standard for high-density inner-city regeneration. This verdict is confirmed by the Housing Design Award 2006 and four other awards it won or for which it was shortlisted.

Abbotts Wharf lies alongside the Limehouse Cut Canal, which the architect has exploited by extending it into the centre of the site as a new spur or basin. The canal basin is now home to four canal boats, and it is adjoined by a paved courtyard that opens on to the public street at its other end, with car parking hidden underground. The result is a traffic-free, water-side piazza in the heart of the high-density development.

Two oblong apartment blocks line both sides of the piazza and rise to eight storeys.

**Top:**
Boxy balconies and coloured panels
dance to a syncopated rhythm.

**Bottom:**
Four housing blocks fit neatly around a new
canal basin and within a triangular site.

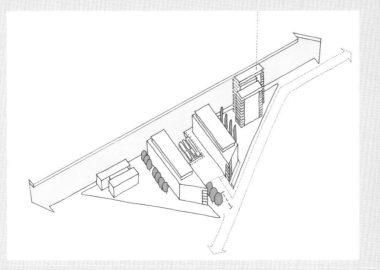

**Left and right:**
Balconies add three-dimensional
modelling to flat facades.

Living
Case Study

83

They are arranged perpendicular to the canal so that all apartments have oblique views of it. And on either side of this pair of oblong blocks stand two point blocks, one four storeys high and containing family maisonettes and the other 13 storeys of smaller apartments.

The blocks have a no-nonsense, industrial feel with crisp, flat elevations in white render and glazed balcony fronts. The elevations are jazzed up by a syncopated rhythm of rendered panels next to windows in alternating terracotta, pink and mustard colours. And, to encourage a sharing, egalitarian community, there is no distinction in appearance or finish between apartments for private sale, shared ownership and affordable rent.

The 50/50 split of private and social housing extended right through the land ownership and development of the project by Telford Homes and East Thames Housing Group. "It was a beautifully conceived and beautifully executed scheme", comments Heinz Richardson proudly. "And it was done in a true partnering manner, where everyone was working for the benefit of the whole project."

# Learning

# Learning

If there was a moment that inspired Jestico + Whiles' involvement in, and approach to, school design, it was perhaps Tony Blair's famous "education, education, education!" speech of 1997.

That so-called "e-cubed" mantra was delivered at the time when the Labour government was setting its sights on lifting standards across the sector as a key priority for its term in office. As a result, government issued a call for consortia to join an education framework in the first Academy programme, where every school would gain a sponsor from the world of business. J+W director Heinz Richardson recalls that the practice wanted to get involved, principally because there might be a lot of work flowing from such a move. But of course there were deeper societal reasons too, more of which later. "For us it would be a leap into the big time in education", he says. Up until that point, the practice had only been involved with small schemes, such as an extension to the Queen Elizabeth Boys' School in Barnet. That scheme came about through an engineering contact of the firm Ellis & Moore, while other jobs in this arena included work for special schools. One such was Fairley House, a school for dyslexic children set up by Daphne Hamilton Fairley, and which was a conversion of an existing building in Pimlico, south London.

But to attack the Academies opportunity properly and with gusto, J+W formed a consortium with a group of large, well-respected names: Davis Langdon, Buro Happold,

Roger Preston and Partners and JL Gibbons Landscape Architects among them. Then, having secured a berth on the framework, J+W was invited to bid and pitch for several schools. A good deal of these were for commercial-led sponsors who brought business acumen and £1,000,000, but in return wanted to see their Norman Foster-designed school emerge, as with Bexley Business Academy, for example. But there was also a reasonably undefined goal to address in creating these academies. "The watchword was transformational education", says Heinz Richardson, with government setting up panels of educationalists to scrutinise the fine detail of the projects coming forward. Happily the chance for J+W came with a project not from an individual but from The Haberdashers' Livery Company, which followed an established, traditional education model. "They knew exactly how to teach—they weren't that interested in educational transformation", says Heinz Richardson. "They just wanted a decent school."

The Haberdashers owned a building in New Cross, south London, which they wanted to expand. Lewisham Council, though, warned them off this course of action, saying that they would instead support the building of a separate scheme on a new site if it duly became a new Academy, to be called Haberdashers' Aske's Knights Academy. The site in question was a very residential corner of Lewisham built as slum clearance housing for dockers. In the interim the 1950s school in this area, Malory, had fallen into

Knights Academy, Lewisham, 2003–2007
Top of the class: The colourful
Haberdashers' Aske's Knights Academy
features a sixth form 'loft' centre and a
keen sense of arrival created via a ramp
leading to a 'heartspace'.

interview for the job, planning to retain an existing sports
hall at its heart, but demolishing it for reasons primarily
associated with the VAT rules of the time. Retaining it
would have made the revenue powers-that-be consider that
the rest of the scheme was an extension, and thus vatable.
"It was more expensive than demolishing a perfectly
acceptable building and replacing it. We didn't have time
to go to Customs and Excise and say 'this is ridiculous',
because it would have delayed the programme." The budget
for the project was lifted by the amount of 'abnormals'
identified with the site, but was hit by bad luck which raised
the cost of work, including the discovery of asbestos and
the concurrent rise in cost for treating it.

J+W's design created a sweeping, curvilinear block called
the learning curve—three storeys of classrooms with a
"heartspace" in its middle which acted as the 'knuckle'
joining two elements, accessed by a wide, inclined
entrance ramp delivering the children to a forum space at
the centre of the action. This helped with controlling the
flow of children in a residential area, says Heinz Richardson,
but also reinforced the notion of arrival. On the top of
this space, J+W designed a sixth form centre, which it
called "the loft", and from which the older students could
enjoy a panorama on the world they would shortly enter,
hopefully better equipped. A large skylight funnel allowed
the enclosed Assembly Hall to get its share of natural light.
Materials include acrylic render and engineering brick at

'special measures' becoming a sink school with an intake
of children mostly from other areas. "They were bussing
in kids from as far away as Hackney to go to this school",
remembers Heinz Richardson. "It was a real take-your-life-
in-your-hands tough school." Transformation needed.

The three-hectare site itself lay in an area called Downham,
surrounded by two-storey housing. J+W won the competitive

1997 "Education, education,
education!" speech by Blair

low level, with the use of a syncopated rhythm of cool blue-coloured glass within the curtain walling. To the west, J+W created a prominent array of solar shading to protect classrooms from afternoon solar gain. Each Academy has a specialism and at Knights this was sports—the claim to fame of the school was that former England footballer Shaun Wright-Phillips went here. So there is also a concentration of up-to-date sports facilities.

"It gave us the experience of working on difficult sites, stretching the budget to work in the best way possible for the school", says Heinz Richardson. "Delivering a low-energy, naturally ventilated school that used heavy-weight construction, and a night time cooling strategy—all those things that we had learnt." It also brought the firm into contact with building bulletins as they applied to school design, and taught the practice how to get the project through the various 'gateways' that the Academy programme threw in its path.

Built by contractor Sisk to a high standard, the school scored top marks, to the extent that the client also commissioned J+W to do some work on its existing site in New Cross,

Opposite and below:
Hatcham College, New Cross, 2007
Dramatic intervention: Hatcham's eye-
catching, cantilevering and popular drama
space, framed in terracotta, contrasts with
the western red cedar cladding around it
and looks out over a new enclosed quad.

area and out towards Crystal Palace. The scheme was completed in February 2007.

Back in Downham, the Academy scheme finished in December of the same year and was similarly transformative where results were concerned, turning it from being a failing school to one which achieved higher standards in a very short space of time, and which is now heavily oversubscribed. The kids themselves—the crucial user group—also loved it. One group of Year 7 boys, asked to write about their impressions, said things like: "My first morning in the new building is probably the best I could have in school", and "the school reached my expectations—and then did a lap of honour", and even "wow—it's like I am in Hogwarts!" High praise indeed.

The success of these schemes meant that J+W could look to reorganise internally, within the office, establishing an education team. "It was a good springboard but it was a baptism of fire because of all the difficulties of doing something on this site and getting it through."

At roughly the same time, J+W won a small Catholic school scheme in Greenwich—St Paul's. This was again a tight site on which a temporary school was also needed before a new Academy could be provided. And again it was an educationally driven solution, where the client was the school—the users—with a clear, distinct vision and expressed needs, rather than a businessman who, as

creating a sixth form building called Hatcham College in which the pupils could be taught in a more collegiate way. The new building at Hatcham creates an enclosed quad like a Cambridge college, with a sustainable agenda driving much of the work. J+W created classrooms, a drama space, two small lecture theatres and break-out spaces, along with a south-facing quad area. The most eye-catching feature, though, is the bold, rectangular, drama studio of terracotta render and engineering brick which contrasts with western red cedar used on the main elevation, cantilevering out over the reception hall, and which frames views over a stepped

Stoke Newington, London, 2010
Skin deep: J+W created a Corten-clad
entrance building with the capacity to
age beautifully, leading on and through
to a rationalised school beyond.

Heinz Richardson puts it, "wanted to change the world".
The school also had a clear, professed desire to appoint a
non-iconic architect. Besides, educational experimentation
is a tricky area, and much time can be lost second-guessing
what "transformational education" might actually mean to
various parties. In the above projects Heinz Richardson is
clear what kind of transformation has been achieved. "It's
about delivering results and outcomes—if that's the right
sort of language; making kids able to have the opportunity to
improve themselves in life."

In Stoke Newington, J+W's work moved on to a scheme
which was redeveloped as part of another major government
programme—this time Building Schools for the Future, which

was overseen by non-departmental public body Partnerships
for Schools. Here though, the successful pitch, in a
consortium with Mouchel Babcock, was for all of Hackney's
schools requirements.

Situated in a conservation area near the Clissold Leisure
Centre, the existing school was a 1967 bush-hammered
concrete Brutalist building designed by Stillman and
Eastwick-Field, but it had groaned under long-term
maintenance and organisational issues, having been built
over a number of levels. The school was looking for a
rationalisation, but one of the main challenges was to
come up with a scheme that did not detract from the
original building, which many people loved, despite its

Stoke Newington, London, 2010
Learning curve: Architectural features
are used to enhance orientation and
wayfinding, while a new entrance block
provides closure to the existing courtyard.

problems. To avoid being either deferential or inappropriate,
J+W came up with a bold, new, three-storey entrance
building, clad in Corten and standing away from the rest
of the school. Corten was used because it had, in Heinz
Richardson's words, "Brutalist qualities without being
brutal", with the propensity to change and age gracefully,
as well as being contemporary and of its time. The block
provides a formal gateway, with a cut-out entrance
penetrating its facade and into the main spaces beyond, as
well as classroom space. Black glazed brick lines the walls
of the interior facade, with offset strip windows above
while, elsewhere, extensive work was done on wayfinding,
using colour derived from a palette inspired by Apple in
some of its products.

**2000** City Academies
Programme launched

Left and opposite:
Stoke Newington, London 2010
Use of colour: Bold use of colour features across the building, especially internally. Colour choices were made with a student working group, who took inspiration from Apple's iPod colours of the time.

Below:
New Line Learning Academy, Maidstone, Kent, 2010
Furthering education: The Maidstone Academy also features extensive use of colour, alongside an unusual teaching environment. The academies here are pioneering ground-breaking teaching methods including the use of large learning 'plazas'.

Clapton Girl's Academy, London 2010
Square root: The design concentrated on
knitting together new and old, reinforcing
a quadrangle space that helps create a
collegiate feel and provides a more defined
circulation route.

The batch of New Line Learning Academies which continued alongside the BSF programme—three in total, built with Carillion on sites across Kent—were a case of pushing the educational envelope. This was in both the manner in which teaching was to take place and also the spaces in which they were to operate. "We talked about educational transformation—this is about as transformational as you can get", says Heinz Richardson.

The school's inspirational Principal Dr Chris Gerry had a very different vision for education from the norm—essentially that it needed to be more like retail, sold to the students in the same way that you might sell a pair of Nike trainers. In other words, the goal was to make pupils want to come to school because it is exciting and different. Thus, the concept evolved of a series of ten flexible learning plazas, rather than classrooms, and almost no corridors.

2002  Staff at J+W send their
Directors to USA

Green shoots: Inspiration for the palette of materials and colours included the Kentish countryside—green glass panels echoing the region's fruit fields.

These plazas are double-height spaces, which when paired together as 'home bases' accommodate a whole year group of up to 120 students at a time, and where the core teaching takes place in an open-plan environment. Specialist learning plazas for science experiments or food technology, for example, are adjacent on the other side of a large central 'heartspace' atrium, which doubles as an entranceway, while the rest of the scheme contains the sports facilities, canteen and so on. In the 1,050 pupil Maidstone Academy, the scheme included a dance/activity centre, lecture theatre, food court, six-court sports hall and shared sixth form facility with the sister Academy at Cornwallis Academy. Referencing the surrounding landscape, the learning plazas are surrounded by a pixelated curtain wall of varying green glass panels—echoing the Kentish fruit field patterns, while the teaching rooms use masonry to reflect the local ragstone, and community facilities are in an interlining volume defined by a terracotta red render. As part of the revolutionary learning strategy here, and borrowing from research done in Harvard, schoolchildren are monitored digitally so that those whose progress is falling behind can be brought up to speed promptly—however Orwellian that sounds.

So, what is it that most appeals about creating learning buildings? Is it their worthiness? The contribution they make to wider society? "I think what's interesting about designing schools is that we all speak from experience, don't we, because we've all been to school", says Heinz Richardson. "So everybody involved in designing or commissioning a school has an experience to bring to it. It's not an exclusive area. It's a bit like designing housing. I think education is extremely important in my own life; it enabled me to become what I have become. Therefore I am passionate about it making a difference—if it makes a difference to one person it is worthwhile. I enjoy it because it is important."

Below and opposite:
**Central School of Speech and Drama,
Swiss Cottage, London, 2006**
Glass act: J+W created a series of studio
spaces stepping down and animating
the street, with different treatments
including vertical white glass and zinc
cladding disguising their scale.

Moving away from schools, and on to further education, the Central School of Speech and Drama project at Swiss Cottage was essentially about making 'boxes' into an attractive part of the city, dealing with large volumes rather than cellular spaces. The big gesture here was to put the circulation spaces on the building's outside so that that element became the 'theatre', bringing the light and drama of people movement to animate the street elevation, through fritted glass. When the school first started it was based in the Royal Albert Hall, moving north and adding several new buildings onto the site over the years. Central wanted a masterplan for developing the whole site, of which the first phase was getting permission for rehearsal spaces. These were the big boxes, which J+W stacked as a series of studio spaces to deal with the geometries along the road at College Crescent and to meet the end of a blockwork wall. The design separates small teaching rooms from larger performance spaces within two distinct boxes, with the circulation spine allowing interaction between building users

at every floor. Materials include vertical alternating white glass with a dark engineering brick base, a bright yellow lift shaft, zinc cladding and distinctive render.

Shifting to the south coast, the Mountbatten nanotechnology job arose following J+W's work on student housing for Southampton University on its Glen Eyre campus, as well as a submission for a new arts facility it prepared for them. But at around the same time, the university's existing nanotechnology lab caught fire following an electrical fault and burned to the ground. So a new one was required, on the Burgess Road site in the town, nestling among new buildings on campus by practices such as masterplanner Rick Mather. Former J+W associate Chris Perry had left the firm to work for CH2M Hill, who specialised in clean room design and recommended J+W for the job. The first challenge was that these are hungry buildings, when it comes to power. The design called for a large power

Below and opposite:
**Mountbatten, Southampton, 2008**
Small is beautiful: This nanotechnology
lab has been held up as an exemplar in
the sector for the way it incorporates
high degrees of technical expertise with
social spaces created in order to foster
more interaction between the scientists.

supply taking up around a third of the site and which generates enough energy for around a third of the city. But at the same time it was committed to getting a BREEAM 'excellent' rating. The next was that the site was adjacent to an SSSI, and under a flight path, potentially problematic for vibrations. J+W interviewed all the professors and ascertained that the university wanted to keep its high level of sponsorship and to show those sponsors the facility at any time. They also wanted the biggest nanotech laboratory in the country—not a contradiction in terms— and to publicise that fact. J+W used a clash of grids outside to generate a circulation space within the building curtilage and natural ventilation for the non-serviced areas. "It's really one of the most efficient laboratories of its type—dare I say it—in the world", says John Whiles. The laboratory walls were glazed so the work within could be

seen from the outside, and there was a general principle of engineering places where the scientists could mix since much of scientific discovery comes from meetings and discussion. "We deliberately made all circulation areas very interruptible", says Whiles. The elegant staircases featured super-sized landings, for example, creating impromptu chat spaces for those chance encounters.

The clean rooms and labs, occupying the two lower floors, are characterised by a Peano-Gosper fractal design etched on the glass panels that enclose the building. This fractal was discovered in research undertaken by Professor Darren Bagnall and Dr Adrian Potts of ECS and Professor Nikolay Zheludev of the ORC. The office and communications space on the upper floors is visually separated by the subtly coloured cladding.

**2005** 'Building Schools for the
Future' programme announced

**2006** J+W study trip to
Amsterdam

**2007** Primary Capital Programme
announced

Mountbatten, Southampton, 2008
Glazed expression: The facade features
a design etched onto glazing and based
on a fractal to help with solar protection,
along with *brise soleil* and dynamic forms
and volumes framing views across a new
south-facing outdoor space.

The scheme was built within three years of the old building having burnt down. It was an important project because there was a complexity and technical expertise involved in putting it together that J+W had never got involved with before. But there was also such a high degree of success in terms of the facility's use and efficiency that when the University of Sydney wanted a similar facility, they came to J+W and CH2M Hill, as did Manchester for its National Graphene Institute. Such has been the manner in which much of J+W's work comes through the door, with repeated successes in most sectors, barring perhaps transport, garnered through word-of-mouth recognition and recommendation. One last example bears this out. The reputation of the Mountbatten project spread so quickly, even to the extent that, on a flight to Cairo, the man in the next seat to John Whiles had even learnt of

**2008** J+W study trips to
Valencia, Cologne, Porto,
Bregenz and Stockholm

**2009** Heavy snow
closes Heathrow

**2010** Students riot over
tuition fees

Mixing bay: An atrium and circulation
spaces are especially generous in order
that groups can meet to exchange ideas,
while other spaces are designed in order
to allow passers-by to see experiments
at close quarters.

its fame. It turned out that the chap in question was in
the US Department of Defence and was travelling to a
nanotechnology conference to keep up with the latest
technologies. Whiles takes up the story: "He said: 'You're
English, right? You should be very proud of the laboratories
you are putting up. I went to one in Southampton yesterday
and I have never seen anything like it'. 'Oh, I said, how
interesting. We built that laboratory.'"

**Top and bottom:**
Media studies: This replacement school for
the inspirational team behind TV's *Educating
Essex* programme concentrated on a radial
plan around a 'heartspace' conceived
in response to the institution's ethos—
providing a flexible and sustainable result.

# Case Study:
# Passmores Academy,
# Harlow, Essex, 2011

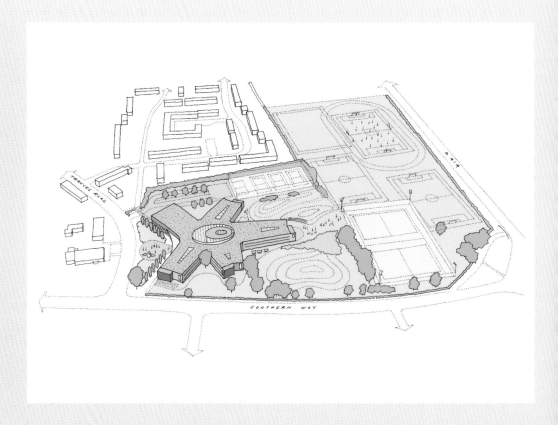

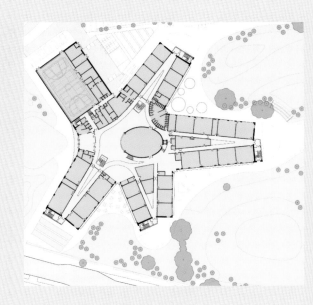

Another school which formerly had issues over behaviour and standards but which has been transformed through architecture is Passmores, which before the change was the subject of *Educating Essex*, the fly-on-the-wall TV series.

"The school behaviour has changed immeasurably—they have so many positive outcomes in so many ways", says Heinz Richardson. Much of this has been down to the teaching staff-turned TV celebrities, including headmaster Vic Goddard, but another key has been the organisational strategy employed in the new design.

The school was an interesting one for J+W as a project because it was procured in a

very different way. This was the Smart East framework, which allowed the local authority, Essex County Council, to commission an architect, contractor and team to design a scheme for an existing school on a new, greenfield site. Perfect.

J+W was interviewed competitively with partner Willmott Dixon, going on to win the job. The existing, badly planned Passmore school was in the New Town of Harlow, with the new site around two miles away on one of the green wedges that run through the place. The old school had many of the usual problems—lots of corridors and hidden areas, cold, poor maintenance, difficult to supervise. So J+W met up with the committed, passionate, inspirational

Top and bottom:
Clad predominantly in timber, the highly
sustainable scheme announces itself to
the community using confident, large-
scaled typography.

Learning
Case Study

103

Below and opposite:
Light heart: The flexible, timber-clad
'heartspace' and radial plan mean that
internal travelling times for the pupils
are improved, and consequently more
time is available for lessons.

teachers on an away-day conference, getting under the skin of the institution's ethos and what sort of school they wanted. At the heart of the school is a raised inclusion faculty, created to help those students who need learning and general support, an 'utterly democratic' move that fits at the centre of a radial plan. Pupils all enter the building through the same entrance into a large, open, toplit 'heartspace' containing assembly hall, dining, library, and from which they can interact and circulate into any of the specialist teaching areas. The 'flower' radial plan model over two storeys is organisationally appropriate but also a good way of integrating a new school building

into a green space which was central to the concept of Sir Frederick Gibberd's New Town masterplan—Gibberd believed these spaces should be for community uses such as schools and sports areas. "By coming up with this form it meant it embraced the landscape and the landscape could come up into the school", says Heinz Richardson. The school operates a house system, denoted in the design by colours, with daylight another important constituent, while the canteen design, with its cashless system, is helping to lift the take-up of school meals by 80 per cent. External spaces between the plan's 'fingers' operate as extra teaching zones, while large parts of the school can be used

by the community, as well as for markets or other events. Another big win is that because of the efficient planning of the school the teaching staff can save three to five minutes on each lesson. The educational outcomes are also being delivered more easily, while poor behaviour has been virtually eliminated, partially because of good sightlines—the teachers can see the pupils at all times. "The behaviour change in the school is marked."

# Theatre

The Hempel, London, 1994
Signature architecture: J+W's acclaimed,
minimalist, 35-bedroom scheme with
interior designer Anouska Hempel involved
reconstructing five Bayswater buildings,
overlooking a graceful landscaped square,
reworked as exterior function space.

# Theatre

'Theatre'—the animation of spaces to give an excited, joyful jolt to their *joie de vivre*—is a major constituent of the Jestico + Whiles portfolio. But it is perhaps most pointed in the practice's work to enliven hotels and cinemas with colour and delight, opening up what was previously an introverted sector to stimulate more mixing in this most mixed-use of building types.

Following the completion of J+W's job at Stukeley Street— an old furniture warehouse for the Savoy Hotel converted into an office with a slender atrium at its core—the scheme was published in the *Architects' Journal*. One reader, who was looking to build a similar atrium in a hotel development, paid particular attention and gave the practice a call. This was Kazuaki Fujita, chairman of Fujita Construction, the biggest firm of its kind in Japan, and the scheme would later become The Hempel, a ground-breaking hotel.

"The chairman of Fujita was a toy collector and he'd seen that the London Toy and Model Museum was up for sale", recalls J+W director John Whiles. "He made a bid by fax and they won it, before anyone from Fujita had seen it." Fujita sent along his cohorts, but the site at Craven Hill Gardens, Bayswater was, in those days not the most sensitive of places for children, frequented as it was by the wrong sort of night time economy. Happily, Fujita had overcome such obstacles before, having experienced similar social and environmental problems with a building

they bought in Santa Monica, where their strategy was to gradually buy up all the surrounding buildings until they owned the street and could then control the area. This was 1990 in London during the slump, but word had quickly got round about Fujita's involvement and its track record. So much so that a backpacker's hotel offered its five other nearby buildings to the Japanese, which they snapped up.

Fujita researched hotels in London and found that only Blakes in South Kensington—founded and owned by Anouska Hempel—was consistently getting 90 per cent occupancy. So they approached Hempel to ask if she would be interested in operating another hotel, which Fujita would build. Hempel agreed, on condition that they let her create a 'minimalist' hotel, and J+W took on the job of creating a new scheme out of the five Bayswater terraced houses. J+W interviewed an Australian architect to be employed by Fujita and who would sit in Hempel's office and work with J+W on liaison. It was the practice's first full experience of working alongside an interior designer. Whiles again: "She was only happy working in spaces she could really see—she couldn't visualise spaces which was understandable in view of all the changes."

The job involved a good degree of detailing Hempel's extraordinary vision, right down to details on stone baths, as well as the creation of wet room bathrooms which were tricky principally because this was a conversion and things had a tendency to move. Then there was the use of 15

The Hempel, London, 1994
Light touch: Great care was taken in detailing
the minimalist corridors, with light features
designed to designate the rooms, and no
door handles to disturb the clean lines.

Opposite page:
One Aldwych, London, 1998
The Grade II listed facade of One Aldwych,
the first steel framed building in London.

and an etched 'running man' on clear glass to skirt round the rules on fire exit signage.

This last even caught the eye of the observant *Sunday Times* journalist AA Gill, who wondered how long that detail had been pored over. Answer: quite a lot. By the time J+W had finished, the scheme's atrium idea—which drew the practice into the job in the first place—could not be accommodated, and neither could Hempel's idea for a suspended swimming pool in that space. J+W suggested a smaller atrium space into which filmic events could be projected from hidden projectors.

Although J+W had been struggling to get public spaces in the building, Hempel insisted that they dig down into the basement, lifting the cost of the project in so doing, since it meant extending the party walls. But it was around halfway through the contract that it was discovered that the garden square—one of only three in London that was privately owned—was in the freehold of the five buildings. J+W created a raised deck flooring system of grass with water features inside it for the square. This meant that the owners could erect a marquee in this space within a matter of around four hours. A new revenue stream was swiftly within The Hempel's grasp: "Suddenly she could do weddings, bar mitzvahs, and fashion shows." Even the final ensemble scene from the Richard Curtis film *Notting Hill* was filmed here. J+W also added business apartments, Fujita's own offices and a refurbished toy museum. But if

centimetre wide, 15 metre long floorboards whose timber was sourced in Oregon and dried in a kiln in Copenhagen before being transported down to the site, only for the carriers to find a scheme so advanced, with partitions up, that they had to be cut down to fit. This notwithstanding, the hotel was filled with neat touches, such as the room numbers projected in light onto the floor, box TVs recessed into cupboards so they resembled today's flat screen sets,

anything, the project's big lesson was how to manage an interior designer, even though the relationship was a good one which still exists today.

Characteristically, given Hempel's contacts and marketing skills, word spread quickly about The Hempel opening, to the extent that during this period J+W were approached by another operator to work on another hotel. This time the client, Scots hotelier Gordon Campbell Gray, was keen to approach the scheme from a services—rather than stylistic point of view. He had backers from India to buy the hotel and convert it into a five-star affair. This was another conversion, here of a Grade II listed building most recently used as a bank that would later become One Aldywch (and which ironically was where Campbell Gray had once been refused an overdraft). "It was a very complicated building", remembers John Whiles, "not just triangular, but each side was concave." J+W took over the job from Conran's (who

made something of a false start) with a brief to prepare a contemporary hotel. In the process it dealt with elements such as a lift shaft immediately at the front entrance by moving the doors, and created the whole of the ground floor as a reception lobby, whose low, 'unofficious', and welcoming desk it could 'hide' behind the lifts. "Our story here is all about the journey; that from the arrival of the car to putting your head on the pillow, we've thought of everything." People sit in the lobby and watch visitors come through, or through large windows onto the 'continental', boulevard feel of Aldwych, or out on the other side towards the Lyceum Theatre.

Built as a printworks and newspaper offices for the *Morning Post*, the Grade II listed building had three basements, and the conversion was hugely intrusive, which involved stripping the building right back to its skeleton. One innovation was the use of vacuum drainage, also used on cruise ships and

One Aldwych, London, 1998
Riveting space: One Aldwych's pool
achieved an industrial feel through the
retention and celebration of some of the
former bank building's structure, such as
its columns.

aircraft, which sucks the waste water up into the ceiling and along to a central plant room. This was a huge liberation to the design team, in a sense allowing them to put bathrooms anywhere. John Whiles again: "It was essential to make this thing work because now we didn't have to have back-to-back bathrooms, we didn't need cisterns for the toilets because it was mains water, we didn't need access cupboards; it really freed us, and broke the mould of conventional hotel design."

One of the other important elements of the scheme was that, in drawing up the response to the brief and arguing that the site was at the centre of London's arts world, J+W also came to the realisation that people do not tend to linger in hotels. The biggest event after shopping is a wash and a change before going out to dinner, or perhaps the theatre after the law courts. This was the justification for making bathrooms bigger than standard, with a walk-in shower as well as a bath.

The rooms for a five-star hotel should be 35 square metres, minimum, but here it was down to 21 in certain rooms, so J+W started playing spatial games to make them feel bigger, using tricks like a 'meandering' wall and carefully placed mirrors. "The doors were made 1,200 millimetres wide so that everything you touched and felt on the journey from the car felt solid and grand and accommodating", adds John Whiles.

Soon, J+W found themselves in the position of putting together a pitch for the interior design of the hotel along with three other interior designers they suggested too, having great fun in the process. Their proposals included white gloves for the doormen which featured one black finger to signify 'number one Aldwych' when they were raised to call a cab. There were also coffee cups where the saucer had just 'NE' on the side, reading as 'ONE' when the coffee was poured in. And there were cocktail glasses continuing the jokey 'one' theme, along with a palette of pale veneers and

**Hilton London Tower Bridge,**
**London, 2006**
The public route through the More
London development to the scheme's
entrance and outdoor spaces.

Theatre

113

wallpapers. After the client's board viewed these proposals in silence, Campbell Gray turned to one of the women in his party. "So what do you think of it?" he asked her. "Well, Gordon", she replied, "it's just what you said, it's fabulous!" Campbell Gray intimated that it was the best presentation they had seen, and suddenly J+W had clinched the job as architect and interior designer. In the event, interior designer Mary Fox Linton who had been selected by J+W to supply many of the specified materials, later took over many of the spaces, but J+W could still experiment with treatments including those around the hotel's swimming pool and gym where the building's steel frame (the first use of such a structure in London) was revealed to communicate the industrial history of the listed building.

Elsewhere, the hotel was the first to have its own private cinema, with a private dining room an added touch. "The Hempel and the Aldwych made our reputations as hotel architects", says John Whiles. On the back of the scheme the practice also started up its own interior design section, and restaurants such as Hakkasan approached the firm, principally because J+W's reputation—for the way it could understand and work with interior designers—preceded it. The Malmaison chain, too, was trying to move on its designs, commissioning J+W to lift its dark timber, quirky portfolio, with seven new schemes. The first was in the Mailbox in Birmingham, the old sorting office with enough space for those attending conferences and needing to show off their wares.

More London also approached J+W to design its first new-build hotel, the Hilton, where it had pitched as architect and interior designer and, where the practice took further the success of what it calls the "lobby culture" used to such good effect at One Aldwych, adding cinemas and other 'extra' spaces. "We were the first architects to make hotels more external and more interactive with their streets", says John Whiles.

**1996** Millennium Dome project
announced

**1997** Bilbao Guggenheim opens

**1997** Damien Hirst opens
Pharmacy restaurant

1998 *Titanic* movie breaks
all records

Opposite and below:
Hilton London Tower Bridge,
London, 2006
Two-faced: The scheme consists of two
interconnecting wings to mediate between
Tooley Street's historic conservation area
on one side, and the contemporary glass
commercial buildings of More London
on the other. Cafes, restaurants and a
banqueting suite animate the building.

The site enjoyed a large footfall, and the local authority wanted the scheme to mediate between the contemporary More London side and the traditional character of Tooley Street on its other, more southerly flank. The masterplan of More London's radial blocks and pathways generated 'slivers' of buildings, of which the Hilton was one of the most difficult. There were height constraints, too, related to a viewing corridor, and the general massing of Tooley Street was another limitation. Inside, J+W concentrated on bringing in natural daylight, opening it up and creating 'theatre' to attract passers-by and customers out from their rooms and onto three levels of public spaces, including a coffee bar, an open ballroom over a restaurant and pre-function area. Horizontal copper and vertical blue glass bands 'break through' the building's exterior. The scheme has one of the Hilton chain's highest levels of occupancy in the UK, attracting banks and their staff to the meeting rooms

or tourists looking for a base for the South Bank, or indeed weddings and fashion shows to its ballroom.

So, what is it about hotels that the practice enjoys? "It is not really the rooms", says John Whiles. "It is rather more the fact that these are mixed-use buildings in the true sense. They are not like an office with a reception, or which then has a canteen—with hotels you are involved with the whole gamut: restaurants, bars, reception areas, banqueting, offices and rooms. A hotel is as much about its finishes and its interior as it is about its exterior, with the operator in fact only thinking about what goes on inside. But they come to us because they see that we can make their buildings a better contribution to the urban form than they normally are. I think they get a bit embarrassed at the repetitive dullness of windows in a terracotta or brick environment which don't contribute anything.... Part of our remit here is to create places and spaces that inspire people."

**1999** Millennium bug feared

**2000** Millennium Dome opens
(and closes)

Top:
Andel's Hotel, Prague, 2004
Bohemian rhapsody: This 280 bedroom hotel
in Prague's cultural and business district
emphasises modern style and comfort.

Bottom:
Andel's Hotel, Berlin 2010
Space and grandeur: This generous reception
lobby recalls grand hotels of times past.

Andel's Prague was the precursor to all this hotel work, built as it was to service a boom in foreign travel, budget airlines and internet bookings. Here, J+W persuaded the client to offer a higher design product because people were making their choices on the internet based on three thumbnails all perhaps within 100 yards of each other, where rooms were going for 80–85 Euros and the flights were going for even less than that.

The brief at Andel's—the Czech word for Angel—was for a three-star hotel which, by the time it was finished, became a four-star offer by lifting its service. The scheme attracted not just tourists from Europe but also film crews and others,

drawn to its flashes of colour and high quality, 'boutique' feel. The scheme was followed by another in Krakow in Poland, again a product of an Eastern Europe being opened up partially by budget airline routes.

Finally the client acquired a large building in East Berlin after an aborted Aldo Rossi-designed mixed-use scheme. The 580 room, castle-like hotel is off-pitch, away from the centre, but was designed as a conference venue with a sky bar and vast entrance lobby, its vivid colours providing an antidote to this rather grey corner of the city, with tenement blocks stretching off into the distance.

**Andel's Hotel, Krakow, 2009**
Cool reception: This 160 room boutique
hotel is situated on a square in historic
Krakow, and subtly references the history
of the locale in its contemporary design.
The reception features warm textured
stone, while reflective metallic shells
enclose the restaurant.

Yas Hotel, Abu Dhabi, 2010
Right formula: J+W's task in Abu Dhabi
was to create an appropriate interior to
suit New York architects Asymptote's
flamboyant grid wrap over the Formula
One track.

A different kind of glamour was the watchword in Abu Dhabi at the Yas Hotel. Built over the Formula One racetrack, it answered a need for a very visible icon when viewed from the air. J+W designed the interior of both wings, while a monocoque bridge was made in a shipyard in Holland and transported by boat. The context within which the design had to work was a difficult trio: the Arabic world, the marine location and Formula One. The interior includes subtle references: Arabic screens around a patisserie area, squid ink colour references, and shapes like shoals of fish. Walls can change colour in their entirety thanks to the application of Corian which has been half drilled and backlit with energy-saving, colour-changing LEDs, enabling the hotel operator

to have very different, coral-reef-like to glacial characters to their spaces throughout the day and into the evening.

In a similar way, the W Hotel is also something of a chameleon, using light to change its character as the day turns into night, chiefly through its exterior. Faced with the disparate architectural context of Leicester Square and environs, an *ad hoc* accretion of Edwardian, Regency, and Georgian, John Whiles found inspiration whilst walking in Paris and spotting a reflection of period architecture in a shop window. Quiet and understated in the daytime, it is as if the building puts on its gladrags and make-up by night with a colourful show of light to match the pizzazz of

**Yas Hotel, Abu Dhabi, 2010**
Track record: The practice responded with a cool, futuristic interior echoing the high-tech world of racing cars, but which also has subtle references to Arabic screens and the marine environment.

**2003** Mick Jagger knighted

Opposite and below:
**W Hotel, London, 2011**
Curtain raiser: The scheme's facade is veiled
in translucent glass suspended off the face
of the building, evoking Leicester Square's
cinematic heritage, its light show contrasting
with Chinatown's vibrant colours.

Theatre

121

theatreland, Chinatown, and glitzy red-carpet premieres.
The scheme's icy cool blue contrasts with the area's red hot
lanterns, while the building's fritted-out veil is penetrated
in the scheme's exterior, framing glimpses of animation
and life within, like a tantalising peep behind the curtains.
Downstairs, and to take advantage of all those premieres, a
retail unit for M&M's pulls in the Leicester Square tourists,
over 100,000 of them per weekend.

Below and opposite:
W Hotel, London, 2011
Mixing it: The ten-storey building houses
retail, leisure and residential accommodation
as well as the 192 room, five-star hotel.

Below and opposite:
PVR Cinemas, Juhu Beach,
Mumbai 2003–2011
Eye max: The Juhu PVR Cinema interior
features stainless steel and air ducts
which resemble fish eyes, within a colour
scheme inspired by Indian saris.

J+W's work with PVR Cinemas uses LED lighting to full effect in order to change the character of its white interior, like a chameleon adapting to different environments. The practice began working on Indian cinemas around nine years ago when there was a huge interest in Bollywood via films like *Slumdog Millionaire*, and exporting a little of the scene to the UK. In return J+W took their European experience in multiplex developments back to India, carefully maintaining the cultural context by introducing popular local cinematic icons throughout the design.

The scheme at Juhu Beach in Mumbai, a well-to-do area of the city, takes on board the fact that cinema-going is a family experience in India, sometimes with three generations and the extended family going along to watch a movie. Added to this, many of the films are epic, with an intermission, meaning the food offer is an important constituent of the design and the operator's profits. The Juhu cinema uses stainless steel and air ducts which resemble fish eyes, within a colour scheme inspired by saris and hot, spicy colours. J+W also helped PVR develop a Gold Class cinema

with its own entrance reclining seats and tables primed for waitress service.

With a different kind of waitress service, back in London, the Playboy Club in the old Rendezvous Casino in Mayfair does share with its distant Juhu cousin an exuberance and theatrical quality, albeit one which is more of a playful tease. J+W produced a scheme with a subtle use of 10,000 Playboy 'bunny head' logo graphics on a set of ground floor screens evocative of an Arabic or Chinese screen, lit internally. The screens are

essentially pivoting shutters which can be rearranged for more privacy or to show a tantalising glimpse of the 'theatre' going on inside the club to the rest of the world outside. Elsewhere, smoke is used as a motif, drawing on the history of the gambling clubs, along with a cigar lounge in an outside space.

J+W is unusual in that it is a combined practice of architects and interior designers and, as these projects have shown, this integrated approach can lead to building designs of great holistic integrity. And, since the vibrancy of any city is

PLUS
jestico + whiles

**Playboy Club London, 2011**
Smoke and mirrors: Smoke is used as a
motif in the interior design including in
the bar area and cigar lounge, drawing
on the history of gambling clubs.

**Playboy Club London, 2011**
Club class: J+W designed this scheme
to allow teasing glimpses of the interior's
'theatre' from the street through ground
floor screens.

to a large extent based on the richness of the streetscape
experience, it is this interplay—between internal and
external design, materials and activity—that allows the
practice to bring a deep, resonant, and vital sense to its
projects and their wider contexts. It is theatre, with the city
as its backdrop.

# Case Study:
# Aloft Hotel, London,
# 2011

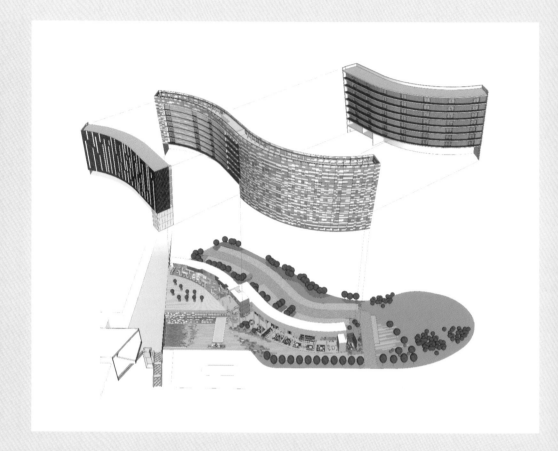

In some ways, the cultural and architectural dockside heritage of the site for the Aloft Hotel at the eastern end of the Excel Centre is incidental to what has happened since. So the hotel—its first in the UK—had to have a certain presence. The standout feature, apart from the serpentine form, is the acid-treated stainless steel facade, with its shimmering, changing, colourful iridescence akin to a fish's skin. John Whiles discovered the material, Rimex, when he was driving through the US, visiting a laboratory in San Diego, and eventually tracking it down in England, of all places. The patina of greens, blues, purples and reds comes from the steel being dipped into an acid bath and,

again the colours change with the passing of the day. The phenomenon is again expressing theatre, and animation where people can stand and watch the colours change, almost going through the whole spectrum in one five minute spell.

Internally, a little of the skin's patina has been brought inside with LED lights in the stone of the swimming pool mimicking the exterior's play of light. Two piazza levels cater for arrivals from the conference centre and for taxi drop-off so the unusual 'dislocation' between the two was handled with another 'joyful' feature—a timber spiral staircase.

**Opposite:**
Your ExCellency: Situated near to the
ExCeL campus in London Docklands the
Aloft Hotel features a convex central spine
flanked by two concave wings.

**Below:**
The scheme is clad in reflective stainless
steel shingles to reflect the day's changing
colours.

**Opposite left:**
A dramatic spiral stair deals with arrivals from the nearby conference centre and taxi drop-off.

**Opposite right and below:**
The light show is continued on the interior of the building with striplights on the stone around the pool.

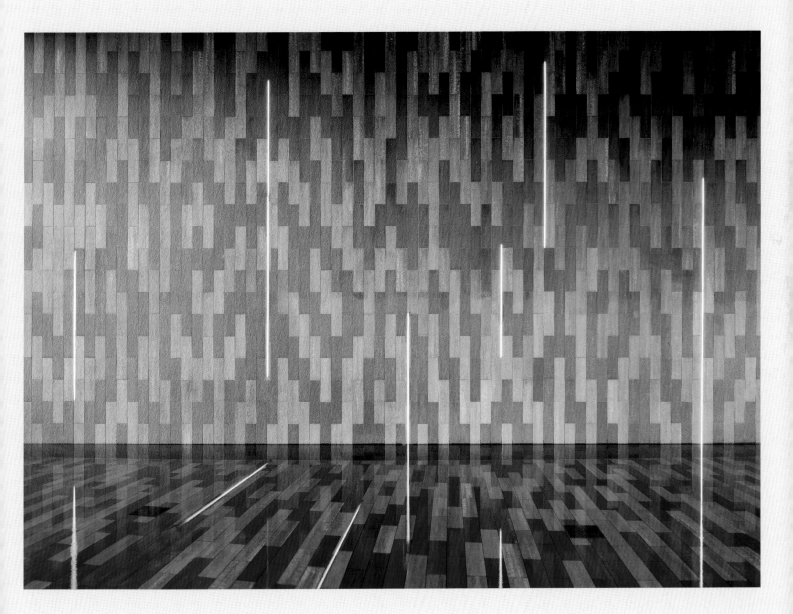

Working

Housing 21 offices, Beaconsfield,
1995–1997
The building form was effectively
moulded by natural patterns of fresh
air and daylight flowing through it.

# Working

The practice eventually graduated from basic industrial buildings, such as at Epsom and Waltham Cross, and office conversions, such as on Stukeley Street, to fully fledged new-build office buildings. In 1995, it was selected by competitive interview for a new head office by Housing 21 housing association, whose chief executive was keen to have a naturally ventilated, low-energy building.

The resulting head office in Beaconsfield is one of those rare buildings whose form was effectively moulded by the natural patterns of fresh air flowing through it. The interior is buoyant and bright in ambience while at the same time dispensing fresh air, daylight and a comfortable temperature in the most natural, efficient and economical manner.

This congruence of architecture, structure and environment was brought about by the new environmental engineering tool of computational fluid dynamic (CFD) modelling, introduced by Cambridge Architectural Research. CFD models digitally calculate air flows and temperatures within a proposed building and plot these graphically on a drawing. The building form can then be manipulated until the most efficient and comfortable pattern is arrived at.

At Beaconsfield, Jestico + Whiles had a pretty clear idea how to steer the CFD-assisted search for optimum environmental form. "The small triangular site gave the building a very good orientation facing northeast and southwest", relates Heinz

Richardson. "You could put cellular offices on the northern side, where they don't get direct sunlight. So they stay cool and are easy to ventilate from one side. Then you put open-plan office space on the south side, where it is passively heated through large windows in winter and you can control heat gain in summer with shading. These office areas are separated by a void that runs along the centre of the building and pops up on top as a continuous laylight with vents. In this way, the central void acts as a lightwell and a clear circulation spine for air and people."

"The CFD model told us that our strategy for natural stack ventilation would work", he continues. "It shows that the space fills up with ventilation air like a bath, the air warms up and rises and pushes the stale air out of the vents at the top. There's no cross-ventilation: the natural stack effect lifts the air gently upwards, so you don't get draughts and papers won't blow around."

Heavy concrete floor and roof slabs play their part by absorbing the heat during day through their exposed ceilings. Then at night the high level vents open automatically without compromising security to purge this heat through the natural stack effect and to let the building breathe.

To get this benign passive ventilation to work, the trick was to carefully correlate the sizes of the 'throat' within the building and the external openings. "If one is too big and

Housing 21 offices, Beaconsfield,
1995–1997
Along the northeast side, a conventional
brick frontage topped by vented rooflights
saves energy and faces a conservation area.

**Housing 21 offices, Beaconsfield, 1995–1997**
Along the southwest side, a window wall admits solar gain in winter but is controlled by shading in summer. The optimum balance of temperature and fresh air was achieved using computational fluid dynamics.

Working                                                                 139

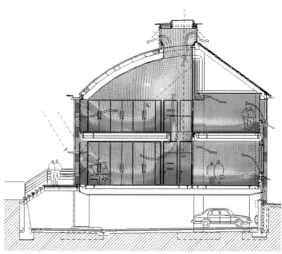

they don't work in tandem, you get an internal environment that is draughty and the building has failed", comments Heinz Richardson. The modern equivalent, then, of the ancient craft of building a fireplace so that the smoke is sucked up the chimney and does not backfire into the room.

Another critical exercise was to design the vaulted concrete roof slab. With structural engineer Price & Myers, the roof slab was painstakingly shaped so that its exposed ceiling would absorb and then release as much heat as possible from the building while assisting the smooth flow of air across it. "There are no intermediate columns, so there's a wide span and the slab is quite thick", explains Heinz Richardson. "And instead of ceiling lights that would interrupt the air flow, there are suspended uplighters."

Ancillary spaces, such as meeting rooms, toilets, stairs and lifts, have been shunted to either end of the building, and car parking tucked underneath in a semi-basement. The

building lies in a conservation area, so it presents warm red brick walls, traditional punched window openings and a tiled, pitched roof to the public street on one side.

The Housing 21's concept as a naturally breathing building was taken up and expanded into an even more ambitious project in Accrington, Lancashire, in 1997. Here the leader of Hyndburn District Council wanted to bring all the council services together into a new town hall that would be the UK's first public carbon-neutral building. In other words, a building that, over a yearly cycle, would generate as much energy as it used and absorb as much carbon-dioxide as it discharged.

To achieve this goal, J+W and environmental engineer, Halcrow adopted a double-pronged approach of reducing as much energy demand within the building as possible, and then satisfying that reduced demand by generating renewable energy on the premises.

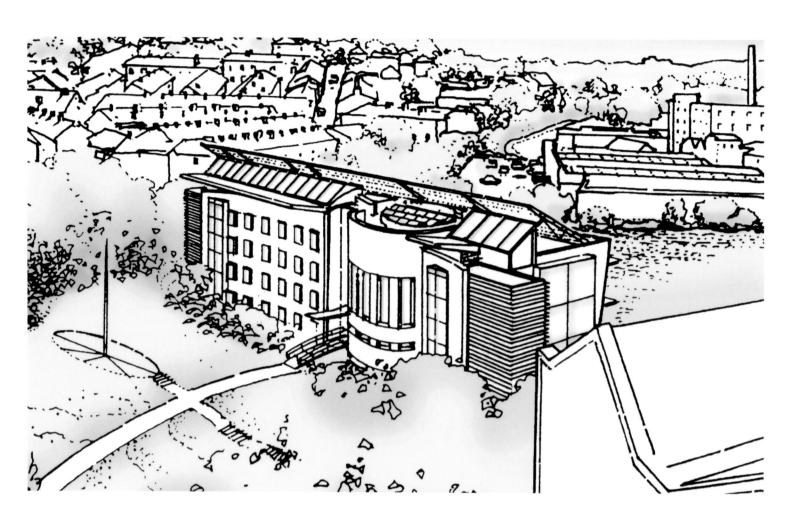

Energy demand at Hyndburn was reduced through the same passive formula as had been used at Housing 21. The building was arranged on similar lines with open plan offices facing south, cellular rooms facing north and a toplit atrium along the middle that would ventilate the building through the thermal stack effect. Then several renewable energy generators were added. The building was to be deliberately sited at the head of a reservoir, where the thermal energy in the water could be tapped by a heat exchanger to warm and cool the interiors as necessary. After that, the stream flowing out of the lake would be harnessed with a hydro-electric generator, and an extensive array of photovoltaic cells bolted on to the roof. Sadly, there was a change of Council before the new town hall could be built and the project was dropped as too expensive.

Two years later, in 1999, the practice won a competitive interview for a new business school for the Open University. The challenge here was not just to design a highly sustainable building, but also one that was attractive enough to persuade academics to abandon their entrenched yet wasteful working practices. (See Case Study on pages 144–147.)

A few years earlier, in 1994, the practice broke into the highly competitive world of high-density office developments in central London. The commission came from the development arm of the Swedish construction giant, NCC, after it had absorbed a team that J+W had previously worked with. The result was an eight-storey corner block of offices above shops and restaurants overlooking Hanover Square, and was the first new-build approval there for 20 years.

**Hyndburn Town Hall, Accrington,
1997–1998**
Natural ventilation is supplied through
the atrium, and renewable energy from
photovoltaics on the roof and a reservoir
at the back of the building.

Working

141

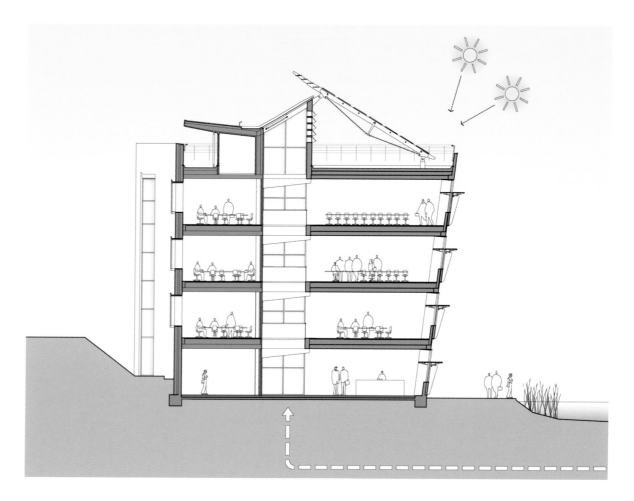

Then in 1996, J+W was admitted into the inner sanctum of
the City of London by Greycoat, the adventurous developer
of Broadgate. The practice won a design competition for a
prominent new office building staged by the developer, for
which it had designed a small office conversion in the West
End years earlier.

The big stumbling block was the building's location right
next to Wren's Grade I listed Monument. "We did endless
studies of how to turn the corner", relates Tony Ling. "And
there was a lot of discussion about 'the fifth elevation', or
the view down from the top of the Monument. The City
Corporation's design and conservation officer, Tony Tugnutt,
wanted the rooftop plant integrated into the building so that
it wouldn't be visible."

In the end, the practice got its design past Tugnutt, who Ling
describes as "ultra, ultra cynical". It also pleased Greycoat
by squeezing in more lettable floorspace than the design
competition's other entrants had done.

Whether on the green fields of Milton Keynes or in the
congested global banking centre of the City of London, J+W
comes up with a design that satisfies all the authorities,
pleases its users and stands the test of time. And in nearly
every case, it delivers a highly sustainable building that is
easy to maintain, absorbs very little energy, and discharges
the minimum of global-warming carbon into the atmosphere.

**Equitable House, London, 1996–1999**
Relating the new building to Wren's Grade
I listed Monument entailed painstaking
reworkings of all five external elevations,
including the roof.

**2001** 9/11 World Trade
Center attack

The corner block has solid walls and rectangular windows to match those of adjoining historic buildings but erupts heroically in a glazed boardroom at the top.

Simple forms and crisp detailing achieve
an understated elegance for this three-
storey academic block.

# Case Study:
# Open University Business
# School, Milton Keynes,
# 1999–2001

When it opened in 2001, the new Business School for the Open University in Milton Keynes was one of the most energy efficient office buildings ever built in this country. Designed with environmental engineer Halcrow, it exceeded the 'very good' BREEAM assessment rating requested by the client and attained the top 'excellent' rating.

Yet even before the competitive interview for the project, John Whiles realised that accommodating the business school's 350 staff posed another very stiff design challenge. "The Open University is a campus with no students, so the average academic staff member is on site for only 30 per cent of the year", he explains.

"But they all want their own room with all their own books around them. And at their campus they occupy long linear buildings where they hardly see each other all day long. The university clearly has an accommodation problem."

So John Whiles proposed the unthinkable: space-saving open-plan offices for academic staff. "One thing you cannot do is to change an academic's approach to life. Not surprisingly, they rejected our proposal. Then we said. 'You're a business school promoting business efficiency: you must practice what you preach.' And then they agreed."

To coax reluctant academics out of their individual bolt holes, J+W adopted several

subtle strategies and wrapped them up in a simple-looking three-storey building on an H plan.

The entrance and communal facilities have all been consolidated into the central bar of the H. That makes it the hub of the school, where all staff rub shoulders with each other as they go about their everyday business.

Staff desks are distributed around the four legs of the H. These are indeed dreaded open-plan spaces, but since all four wings are cul-de-sacs with no through traffic, they are nearly as quiet and undisturbed as cellular offices.

Finally, a secret default option has been built into the office wings. Since the wings

**Top left:**
Natural ventilation circulates efficiently
through hollow concrete floor slabs.

**Top right and bottom:**
The central hub of the H plan contains
shared facilities where staff can meet
and chat.

FLOOR SLAB DETAIL

CROSS-SECTION

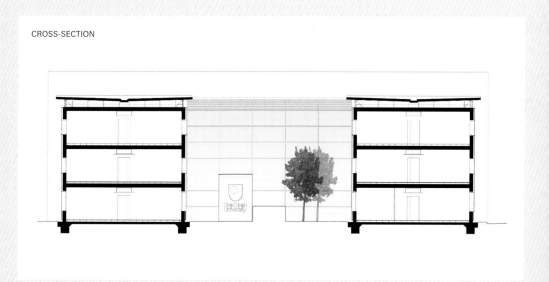

UPPER LEVEL PLAN

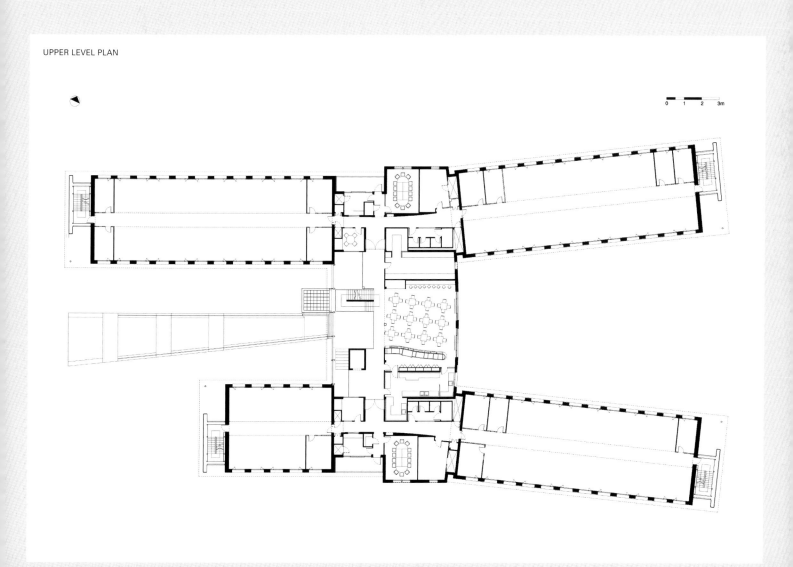

0  1  2  3m

are only 12 metres wide with no internal columns and ample daylighting from both sides, the open-plan interiors could easily be switched on demand back to traditional cellular offices lining a central corridor.

On the energy-saving, sustainability front, the building was just the second in the UK to adopt proprietary hollow Termodeck floors. The hollow concrete floor planks double as ventilation ducts, through which all the building's fresh air is supplied and stale air is extracted. The air flows through the floor rather than merely wafting over the surface exposed to the room, and this gives it more contact with the concrete. It can therefore make fuller use of the inherent thermal mass of the concrete by absorbing heat from it in cold weather and off-loading

heat to it during night time cooling and when the interiors get too stuffy. In winter, extra heat is mechanically recovered from exhaust air and transferred to incoming air by a heat exchanger, making perimeter radiators unnecessary.

As well as reducing energy demand substantially, Termodeck floors are renowned for effortlessly maintaining stable, comfortable and fresh internal environments. Added to that, the Termodeck system has been specially adapted to make the Open University building flexible. The primary ducts supplying and extracting air from all the hollow concrete planks in each wing have been grouped together above a central suspended ceiling. It makes no difference to the central suspended ceiling and its primary air ducts whether the

space below is left open-plan or fitted out with cellular office partitions either side of a central corridor. The building's other sustainable features include a large underground tank where recovered rainwater is stored before being used to flush toilets. And occupants can control their own workplace lighting from their desk with just a few clicks on their PC.

In appearance, the building emanates cool efficiency in its rectilinear forms, crisp detailing and white-rendered walls with strip windows. Elegant touches have been added in the recessed cornice, slatted oak end walls and slender steel corner columns. Then inside the building, the hub sparkles to match with plentiful glass, polished surfaces and fresh colours.

**Opposite:**
At the ends of the four wings, slatted timber screens offer veiled views in and out of glazed staircases.

**Below:**
Staff kitchenettes and small balconies are included at either end of the central hub.

Plus

# Plus

With its irrepressibly let's-have-a-go attitude, Jestico + Whiles has tackled a diverse miscellany of projects over the years. This has led the practice in one direction to the heavy engineering world of transport infrastructure, and along another route to indulge in a few fun, often carefree projects.

As for Tom Jestico's own new-build house, it just fell into his lap out of the blue in 1987. Or at least the site did. "There was a director of a well-known furniture company I was talking to", Tom Jestico relates. "One day, as he was getting into his car, a man came up to him and said: 'I've found this site in Putney and I'm looking for an architect. Could you suggest one?' And the furniture director replied: 'Why not try Tom Jestico?' because that's who he'd been talking to ten minutes before. So we designed a house, obtained planning consent and prepared working drawings for him. And then he told me he'd met a lady from California, and very soon he went off to live with her. But he hadn't actually bought the site: he'd just strung the vendor along."

"Now, the person who owned the site lived next door, and he had Parkinson's Disease. He had to sell the site quickly: he needed the capital to pay for 24 hour care. He said: 'I'm fed up with being messed around. I'm putting the site up for auction in two weeks time.' I said: 'I'll give you the money.' So I bought the site from him." And within less than two years, Jestico had designed and built his own family house there. (See Case Study pages 156–159.)

A decade later, in 1999, J+W found itself drawn into the fantasy world of *Peter Pan*. Two years after the sudden death of Princess Diana, a magical children's playground was created in her memory next to her former home, Kensington Palace. The Diana Memorial Gardens were conceived as a wonderland on the theme of Sir JM Barrie's children's classic, a favourite of Diana, and incorporating a pirate ship, wigwams, and play sculptures, all set in what would become lush woodland.

The practice was called in by a near neighbour, the landscape architect Land Use Consultants, to design a building containing mainly children's toilets. It was modelled on Wendy's secret underground house in the story, though it is not actually underground but rather under a grassy mound supported on an in-situ concrete shell. Continuing the gardens' magical effects inside are shafts of sunlight shining down three overhead funnels and intriguing shadows cast by figures of pirates and Indians etched into the glass doors.

One year later, in 2000, the practice was given an opening into China, again by Land Use Consultants. The location was the global financial powerhouse of Pudong that was shooting skywards on Shanghai's waterfront. The project itself was perhaps not quite so high-powered: it comprised a series of gateway buildings for a public park masterplanned by Land Use Consultants.

**Diana Memorial Gardens, London, 1999–2000**
Toilets to this children's playspace were modelled on Wendy's secret underground house in JM Barrie's classic fantasy, *Peter Pan*. Shadowy pirates and Indians join in the fun.

Pudong Park gateway, Shanghai, 2000
Wavy roof canopies in seamless steel
sheet evoke a Chinese dragon and were
inexpensively manufactured at a local
steel rolling mill.

"There was no written brief at all", recalls Tom Jestico. "So we came up with a few conceptual ideas and sent them off. Then after six months we received an invitation to go there with a structural engineer. We had conceived this building in copper, steel, bamboo and plywood. But when I arrived they said: 'No, no, no. Copper and plywood are too expensive. We're going to build the whole thing out of rolled steel sheet.' And there was a shipyard with a steel rolling mill nearby. So we revised our sketch design and they produced full working drawings, all exactly as they said they would, within just five days."

In the completed buildings, the rolled steel sheet has been fittingly expressed in seamless, wavy roof canopies meant to evoke a Chinese dragon. Beneath the canopies are glazed structures containing ticket office and other accommodation. Pudong Gateway was the first project the practice tackled using three-dimensional computer-aided design. Did it also give the practice a foothold in the world's biggest construction market? "A small toenail-hold", says Jestico. "It didn't lead to any other projects in China."

Seven years later, in 2007, the practice was invited to come up with another quick, tiny, and highly unusual design concept, this time closer to home. It was a limited design competition for a footbridge across Paddington Canal Basin, and there was no engineer involved. Perhaps the invitation from Chelsfield was by way of consolation for three different residential schemes that J+W had designed nearby for the developer but had all been superseded by office schemes. In the competition, J+W had fun conjuring up a bizarre yet perfectly feasible concept for a pivoting bridge. But they were beaten by sculptor-cum-engineer extraordinary, Thomas Heatherwick, with an even more bizarre roll-up bridge.

**Paddington footbridge, London, 2007**
In this ingenious yet unbuilt concept, either wing of a hollow V-deck fills with water to pivot the footbridge to open or close across the canal.

Plus

153

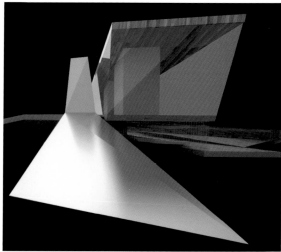

**West Ham station, London, 1999–2000**
Faced with very difficult site access to
a fully operating station, J+W devised a
modular kit of parts for a platform canopy
that could be largely prefabricated off-site.

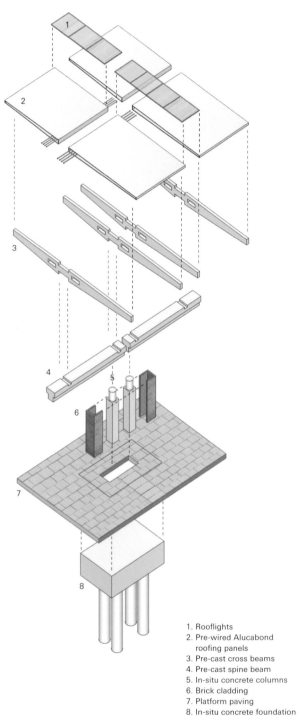

Also in London and the southeast of England, the practice has been more successful in picking up transport infrastructure projects, all in congested urban areas. Since 1991, it has tackled 14 major projects, from the refurbishment of London Underground stations and bus stations to resuscitating a derelict overground line and building Borough Viaduct.

Transport infrastructure can by its nature be mind-numbingly complex. Perhaps J+W's most clear-cut project was the design of a new platform and ticket hall at West Ham station on London Underground's District line. It was carried out with civil engineer, Whitby Bird, in 1999–2000.

The biggest obstacle at West Ham was very limited site access, as the station remained open, the platform was narrow, and trains were continually running past on either side. Yet J+W turned this adversity to advantage by adopting that perennial favourite of architects, a modular kit of parts that could be prefabricated off-site and then quickly assembled on-site.

The new canopy needed new supports which, in turn needed new piled foundations to be driven deep into the ground. On top of the pile caps, the platform was renewed with concrete slabs, and pairs of steel columns erected. At the column heads, a linear primary beam was slotted in and, above that, a series of shallow Y-shaped cross beams, all in precast concrete. The pairs of spindly steel columns were later encased in more substantial brick piers.

1. Rooflights
2. Pre-wired Alucabond
   roofing panels
3. Pre-cast cross beams
4. Pre-cast spine beam
5. In-situ concrete columns
6. Brick cladding
7. Platform paving
8. In-situ concrete foundation

West Ham station, London, 1999–2000
Gaps left between pairs of panels
were glazed over to add rhythm to
the long canopy.

Plus

155

Then came the roof canopy itself. It was supplied as a series of sandwich panels with aluminium-faced composite board below, plywood and roofing membrane on top, and with recessed striplights, intercom loudspeakers and cabling already fully installed. Narrow gaps were left between pairs of canopy panels and, as a finishing touch, these gaps were glazed over to articulate each structural bay and to add rhythm to the long, continuous sweep of the canopy.

In this way, the whole platform was neatly and elegantly renewed in what Tony Ling calls a "plug-in and play modular system".

The four miscellaneous projects in this chapter demonstrate the gusto that J+W applies to all its projects, whether they are one-off houses on tight sites, fantasy wonderlands for children, or deadly serious matters of urban transport.

# Case Study:
# Jestico House,
# London, 1987–1989

In 1987, Tom Jestico and his wife, Vivien Fowler, a practicing interior designer, bought a former kitchen garden surrounded by high brick walls in Putney, west London. On it, they designed and built a simple, single-storey glass box to house themselves and their two sons. A glass box, mind you, with the purest Modernist pedigree that stretches back to Charles and Ray Eames' own house in California of 1949 and Mies van der Rohe's Farnsworth House in Illinois of 1950. Like the Farnsworth House, it even floats above the ground with a timber deck around it.

Jestico himself is more prosaic about his design rationale. "It was designed on the principal of a 1960s office block. You have the core in the middle and habitable rooms all round the perimeter. It has a steel frame on regular 3.9 by 3.9 metre square bays, and a dead flat roof."

Procuring this simple glass box, however, proved to be far from simple. Wandsworth Council's planning officer was aghast, and his recommendation for refusal was only overturned after Tom Jestico persuaded the committee chairman to visit the site and see for himself that the house would be entirely hidden from public view by the high garden walls.

Then the council's building control officer said that the all-glass walls would lose more heat than was permitted under the regulations. And that was even using sealed double-glazed units with a low-emissivity coating to further reduce heat loss. Now, this is where the floating floor played its part. "The regs at the time didn't allow you to count a ground floor as an external element that contributed to the thermal insulation", says Tom Jestico. "So I explained to him that if you raised the floor it would be an external element. And he said: 'If you say so, I'm sure you're right.' We got building regs approval."

After that, building contractors were likewise turned off by the unorthodox residential construction. Only one quotation was submitted, and that was too high. So the couple appointed trade contractors and managed the construction themselves.

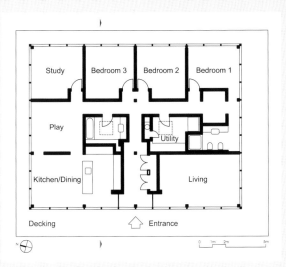

Here, the modular design came to their assistance, as the made-to-measure components required little more than bolting together on site.

"We started work on the house in May 1989 and moved in in October", recalls Tom Jestico. "Since then, it's been a hugely enjoyable house to live in." And for what is still no more than a simple glass box, a most elegant one at that.

As for the two family cats, they found a particular affinity with the raised floor. "You couldn't put a cat-flap in a sealed double-glazed door", explains Tom Jestico. "So we put the cat-flap in the floor opening down to a route out underneath the house. On the day we moved in, I shoved both cats through the cat-flap, and they never needed showing again."

Progress

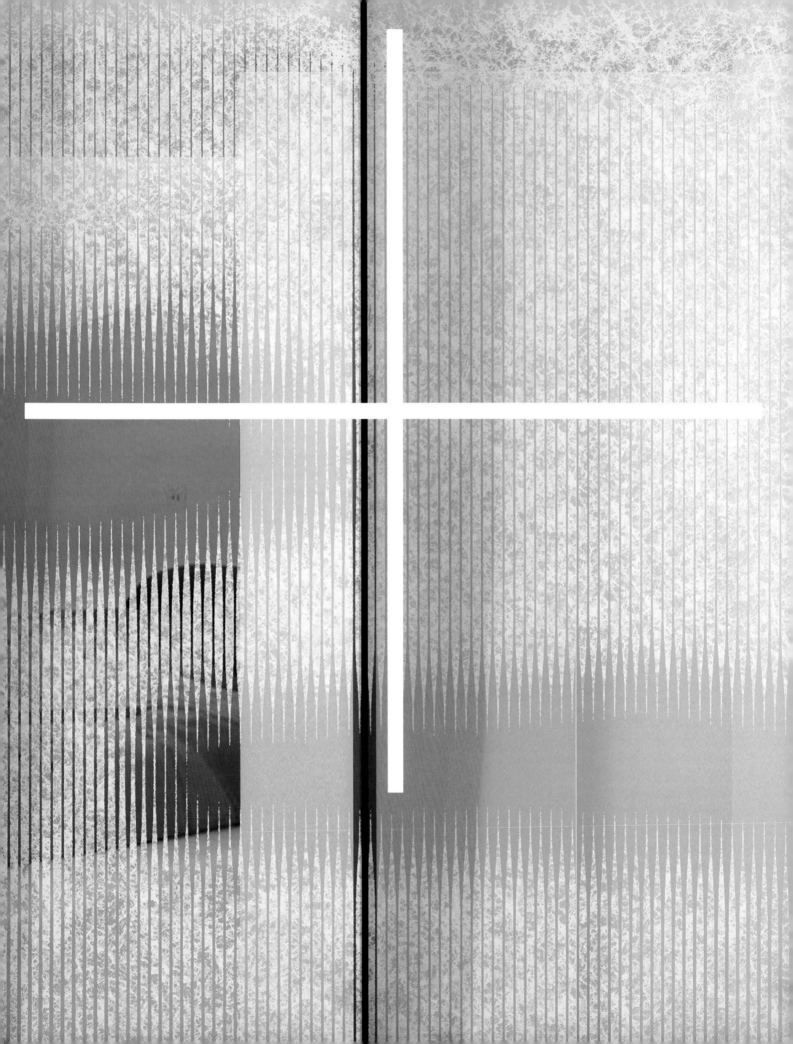

**Borough Market, London, 1999–ongoing**
On track: This complex, long-running
scheme includes under construction plans
for a new glazed market hall building
which opens up views of Southwark
Cathedral and provides a new presence
on the high street.

# Progress

By definition, a practice's work in progress links its ethos and oeuvre to the way it either wants to, or is forced to, evolve in the future. In Jestico + Whiles' case, the outlook is a rosy one, bucking the economic trend with a healthy crop of ongoing, sizeable, and important projects. And, like much of its portfolio, it is the result of both happenstance and hard work.

These principles—being in the right place at the right time, serendipity, having the right application and contacts, and

building up an expertise in a building sector which might bear fruit in repeat business—are evident in J+W's work on laboratories, particularly in nanotechnology. Small is clearly beautiful.

The success of the practice's Mountbatten Building at Southampton University led directly through word of mouth and recommendation to similar schemes in Sydney and Manchester. "It's taken us off on a whole technological journey, where we are delivering competently", says John Whiles. "But that is how we have always got work. We are just invited onto hotels and suddenly we have got hotels, and the hotels invited interior design, and we're now having housing people coming to us because of our interior design."

The one anomaly in this pattern, where work has not come through quite so readily, is in transport. But one project where J+W's work has had long-running involvement that stretches on into the future is the unfortunately named (given its timescale) Thameslink 2000 project at Borough Viaduct.

This was a complex project designed to stop bottlenecks of trains and double their throughput into Charing Cross and London Bridge stations from the south. It necessitated building a new viaduct to lead these trains into the centre; demolishing buildings; carefully taking down the market's

Borough Market, London, 1999–ongoing
Shard shadow: The scheme—part of the
wider regeneration of the London Bridge
area—under construction.

Progress

163

**National Graphene Institute,**
**Manchester, ongoing**
Low carbon: Designed primarily for the
research and commercial application of
graphene, the scheme will include space
for commercial organisations, and with
early thoughts tending towards having
two clean rooms, one on top of the other.

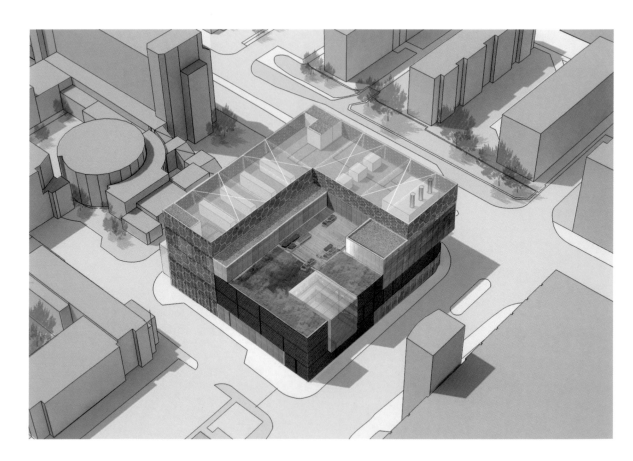

historic cast iron structure; moving the market out
temporarily while building work went on and then back in,
and creating a new bridge across Borough High Street. The
bridge has gone in, two buildings have been demolished,
two have been rebuilt and the third more contemporary
scheme is on the way. The whole project involved close
working with Network Rail, main contractor Skanska and
civil engineer WS Atkins, and so is very much a 'knitting'
job, says John Whiles, with little in the way of 'brave new
architecture'. But a jokey film made by J+W staff, where
they interviewed people passing by the site—pinpointed
one of the key problems of the scheme; that the Viaduct
has no identity. The politics of the famous market and the
strength of feeling that any tampering with it evoked were
also part of the equation.

Following two public inquiries, J+W created replacement
buildings, acoustic barriers, a new canopy for the temporary

market, and designs for a new glazed market hall building
that is 50 per cent bigger than its precursor, opens up
views of Southwark Cathedral and gives it a new presence
on Borough High Street. But the whole project—not
to mention those eased bottlenecks—is some way off
completion, with tracks, signals, electrics and London
Bridge station's redevelopment still to come.

Nanotechnology, though, is now no small fry in J+W's
wide and varied portfolio. The National Graphene Institute
in Manchester is one job in progress which is, like many of
these particular science building projects, geared towards
attracting and retaining the best minds in the business. In
this case, the people in question are two Russo-British,
Nobel Prize-winning physicists, Andre Geim and Konstantin
Novoselov. They won the 2010 Nobel Prize in Physics for
their work on graphene, a honeycomb lattice allotrope
of carbon which is only one atom thick—or one three

Eureka moments: A double-height break-
out space connects two floors of labs
and offices, and features a sliding glazed
'door' overhead.

millionth of the thickness of a sheet of paper. This wonder material conducts electricity six times the speed of copper but without 'jumping', so has potential uses in medicine, telecommunications, microelectronics, biomaterials, energy and a host of other applications, thereby attracting the interests of the Sonys and Samsungs of this world.

The building is being conceived specifically for R&D on graphene with industry input. Such is its import that Treasury secretary George Osborne met the scientists, and promised £50 million to create the scheme even before

a feasibility study was drawn up. "We had never heard about the project", recalls Tony Ling. "But one day I said, why don't we do some research and see who is building this type of facility—nanotechnology research buildings." When they discovered the Manchester project, Tony Ling wrote to the university. But he was quickly rebuffed because the project had to go through strict procedures laid down by the Office of Government Commerce, and 12 major project managers and quantity surveyors had already pre-qualified. To get involved at this stage, J+W would have to join up with one of the 12 teams already on the

CEAC Cuba, Havana, ongoing
High Fidelity: The reception building features
a curved oversailing roof made of reinforced
concrete to announce the campus.

OGC's framework. Just one of the 12 prospective partners, quantity surveyor EC Harris, responded positively to Tony Ling's letters. Services engineer CH2M Hill, also from the Mountbatten Building, became technical architect and M+E engineers. Yet despite the late start with just 18 days to put together a detailed bid, the team won the commission. No doubt the previous experience of J+W and CH2M Hill at Southampton and Sydney stood in their favour.

The site in Manchester is small, and sits alongside other schemes on the university's science campus. Early design thoughts are that the building should be four or five storeys, perhaps with two independent cleanroom spaces, one on top of the other, or the cleanroom located below ground on bedrock to minimise vibration risks.

Another laboratory scheme underway is in Cuba, a country whose leading scientific export is microbiology. This state-owned industry is being championed by Fidel Castro junior, Dr Fidel Castro Diaz-Balart, who is the acclaimed nuclear physicist son of the former President and the scientific advisor to the Cuban Government. J+W is designing a main reception building on a new scientific campus on the outskirts of Havana, where companies will be encouraged to sit alongside the research departments.

The brief is for a 2,000 square metre iconic building housing a 180 seat lecture theatre, cafe and terrace, offices, ancillary accommodation and links to adjacent laboratory buildings. The design features an oversailing curved reinforced concrete roof to announce the entrance to the campus and provide solar shading and thermal mass. A dramatic conical form housing a lecture theatre penetrates this roof, while internally a naturally ventilated double-height space contains the entrance foyer and cafe.

Our plan in Havana: The scheme includes
a lecture theatre at its heart, accessed
from a number of levels.

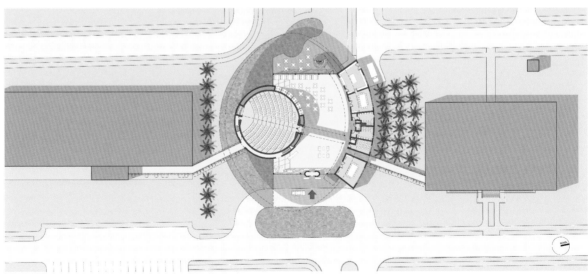

Greenwich Millennium Village,
Greenwich, ongoing
Street life: The masterplan concentrates
on the creation of a place with a rich
variety of building types, public spaces
and routes through.

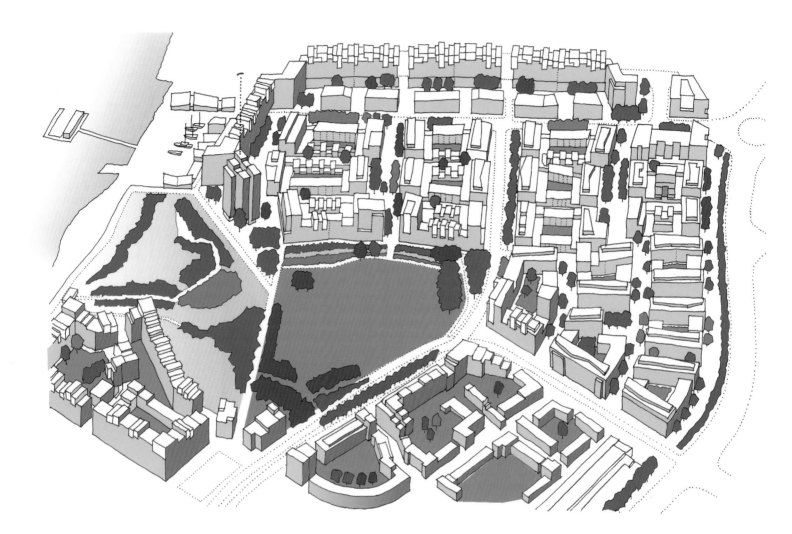

As well as nanotechnology labs, housing remains a large concern for J+W, perhaps best exemplified in the practice's work in Greenwich. The masterplan scheme proposed at Greenwich Millennium Village, on the peninsula, was subject to myriad site challenges, chief of which is high levels of noise from the nearby aggregates wharf, dredger and roads. The existing Ralph Erskine-designed village's early phases have spawned a residents' community with a strong sense of ownership. Collaborating with Peter Barber Architects and Studio 54, J+W's competition-winning scheme for 1,800 new homes on a 24 hectare site has similar aims, as an exemplar of urban design formed from a mixture of townhouses and apartments laid in traditional street patterns

and linked by open squares. The plans include a crèche, community building, shops, restaurants, cafes, bars and workspace, distilling and echoing Erskine's architectural typology and creating a place with rich variety and routes through. The noise from the aggregate wharf will be shielded by an 11-storey terraced block of three buildings connected by glazed screens, which allows for low-rise buildings with natural ventilation elsewhere on the plot.

"We were trying to focus the scheme not around the architecture and the buildings but the spaces they created", said Heinz Richardson. Emphasis is placed upon pedestrian and cycle movement, with parking reduced to 50 per cent.

Community living: The plan includes an
11-storey 'wall' of accommodation to
act as an acoustic buffer from a working
wharf for the benefit of the rest of the site.

**High Street Stratford, London, ongoing**
High hopes: The 30- and 15-storey
Stratford project has been designed as a
'gateway scheme', signalling the border
between Newham and Tower Hamlets
in London.

High Street Stratford is another housing project which had to deal with another particularly noisy and dirty urban challenge next to the intersection of two very busy roads. The scheme consists of two towers—one at 30 storeys, the other at 15, with an off-site contribution on social housing. The irregular geometry for the buildings came from the need to maximise daylight and views, with a car park linking element at second floor which meant that homes could

escape the level of the flyover where the A11 Bow Road crosses over the A12 Blackwall Tunnel Northern Approach. And, because the boundary between Newham and Tower Hamlets runs nearby, the area looks like a gateway, creating a justification for going tall, says Heinz Richardson. The units feature wintergardens, and the building also features community workshop uses and rooftop gardens, while the buildings step down to the canal to complete the picture.

**2011** Summer riots

**2011** Government pledges
£50 million towards Graphene
development

**2012** UK back in recession

**High Street Stratford, London, ongoing**
Fly over: The geometries of the plan have
been generated by the need to maximise
light and views for the residents, as
well as for users of the workshops and
rooftop gardens.

Progress

171

# Case Study:
# Australian Institute
# of Nanoscience,
# Sydney, ongoing

The Australian Institute of Nanoscience in Sydney is a little more advanced in programme than others in this section. Jestico + Whiles was invited to bid, again on the strength of the Mountbatten Building, and struck gold by joining up with Architectus, a Sydney-registered partner architect which had already completed a sensitive microscopy lab. The two UK teams on the shortlist, J+W and Grimshaw, were offered interviews over the internet. "But if I were the university I wouldn't hire someone just from a fuzzy webcam interview", says Tony Ling. So plane tickets were duly bought and the trip was made, along with CH2M. The quick-thinking investment paid off. The impetus to build the scheme is again based around science brains, the Australians having hired some Harvard hotshots. J+W's scheme is organised around a quiet research courtyard and dramatic double-height 'teaching' atrium, with a flexible and modular approach adopted for the research areas to allow for future developments in nanotechnology, tool delivery and move-in routes.

"These sorts of buildings must be clean, vibration-free environments, with temperature control, and no electro-magnetic interference (EMI)", says Tony Ling. "But not only do you have to avoid external EMI, a lot of the equipment inside the building actually generates EMI itself. Clean rooms are very expensive elements—one square metre can cost £9,000—because they are so service-heavy, with so much air having to be circulated, filtered and heated to the right temperature."

Opposite:
Clean rooms: The design is organised
around a quiet research courtyard and
a dramatic double-height 'teaching' atrium.

Below:
Trailblazer: The £45 million project aims
to establish Sydney as one of the world-
leading centres for nanoscience research.

**Opposite:**
The double-height atrium provides circulation,
natural daylight and views into the heart of the
teaching space.

**Below:**
Chance encounters: The design concentrates
on providing mixing spaces and the ability
for scientists to see and be seen in their
working environment.

But these are not windowless boxes—the trend is towards visibility, with the scientists being viewed roaming in their natural habitat, as it were. "You've got to be able to see into the clean rooms so that they can walk their sponsors and other commercial people around", says John Whiles, "and those working in the laboratory should see and experience the passing of the day at the same time."

John Whiles adds that the need for interacting, break-out spaces between researchers is another emerging trend continued here as a progression from the extra-deep landing areas J+W designed on the stairs at Mountbatten in Southampton. A further step in this direction is that the cafe is located at the hub between new and existing buildings with direct access to the lively 'Physics' courtyard.

# Jestico + Whiles
# in the Future

Looking to the future of the practice, John Whiles says: "If one were leaving the practice to the next generation, it would be, if not a fabric, a spirit of place where people continue to do what you were doing yourself. What I like to think we do here is give everybody freedom within the team." Heinz Richardson agrees, adding that the practice is an 'organic' one, which has "grown to accommodate the world around us".

In a sense, Jestico + Whiles has prepared itself for the future by creating a structure and culture that allows progression in various different directions. How, then, will the next generation of directors avail themselves of this liberal structure and culture to take the practice into the future?

In response to this provocative question, here are the visions of the practice's seven associate directors.

**Sean Clifton**
"What I want for the practice and where it will be going is to ensure that we have large-scale, inspirational projects in at least seven different countries at all times in the future. All projects will be uniquely contextual, especially as we extend our portfolio into outer space. Prague and London will further establish ourselves (maybe with a permanent presence) in India and across Asia, and we will be invited on a regular basis to take part in international design competitions for public buildings, private developments and large-scale masterplans.

We will be the architects of choice across Europe, India and Asia, and will design the first hotel to be located outside of the earth's atmosphere."

**Andrew Costa**
"I see us becoming more and more influenced by art and artistic expression using colour, texture and fine detailing within our projects. I think our approach is like a Japanese painted lacquer box, it has a real depth, which is made up of layers and layers of thought and process, yet what is seen and experienced is the final quality and finish. As developers and clients look for that something extra-special and extraordinary, I believe they will be looking for practices that are able to be bold, yet are confidently skilled and provide this additional depth in design. Where do I see us in the future?

Swimming against the tide, and being better for it."

### James Dilley

"In the 18 years since I joined, J+W has earned a wide reputation for excellence in hotel design, for architecture, interior design and both disciplines combined as a single service. This expertise continues to attract clients in a widening area. We have current projects in The Urals, Russia and in India, and opportunities as distant as The Crimea, Myanmar, East Timor and Papua New Guinea. Interior design inquiries include a floating casino in international waters and a luxury retail mall in Australia. Each one of these is a special project. My target is to continue the practice's momentum in delivering special projects, in special locations, wherever they might be."

### Jude Harris

"I want the practice to continue to evolve and prosper with the same spirit of adventure, ambition and affinity that has characterised my experience over the past 14 years. I hope that we can continue to value all staff and the contribution so vital to a team approach, which eschews the notion of the individual designer. I want the practice to be a genuinely nice place to work, rewarding individuals both financially, but also creatively and intellectually.

In an unpredictable future, I hope we will continue to maintain our diversity of projects, an aptitude for all design challenges, with a passion and commitment underpinned by a sophisticated base of knowledge, experience and professionalism."

### Eoin Keating

"I want J+W to develop the egotism and arrogance that it clearly lacks. We've been held back for too long by being a great place to work, attracting some really talented people and producing some really good buildings along the way. That's all very well, our clients might be happy, but where are the things that really matter? Like executive facilities for senior staff? A box at Wembley? Seats in the House of Lords? Things have GOT to change."

### Ben Marston

"I am very proud that since day-to-day operational control of our practice was passed down to the Associate Directors several years ago, we have built arguably the most successful team in the practice's history. Some of the work we are currently doing is amongst the most challenging, yet best we have ever done.

With such a talented team we have every opportunity to make the practice even more successful. But we need to be cautious that any expansion is measured, reflective of our core values, and achieves design excellence."

### James Tatham

"The nature and volume of our work will continue to evolve with time. We can convince ourselves that we direct a course to achieve our personal and common goals, but in reality we are subject to influences beyond our control. What must remain is the spirit of Jestico + Whiles. Hard to define, it's not just an approach to design or the way we work, it's the relationships we form with those around us. Qualities of respect, inclusion, friendship and enjoyment; present when I first joined, these remain today and would I hope continue into the future."

# Overview

**Left to right:**
Archetypal J+W architecture:
Open University Business School, 2001.

Shape moulded by passive ventilation and
daylighting: Housing 21 HQ, 1997.

Five-star hotel interiors liberated by vacuum
drainage: One Aldwych hotel, 1998.

# Overview

"We design simple, rational, pragmatic, contemporary buildings." So runs the mantra recited by Jestico + Whiles' founding and current directors.

All perfectly true. The directors accept that they are not in the iconic super league of architects but rather in the British contemporary mainstream league. Yet they pride themselves in being firmly at the top of this league, producing buildings of consistently high standards in all aspects and on less-than-iconic budgets. More than that, mainstream with flashes of inspiration that can transform working buildings into what John Whiles calls 'theatres' of spectacle and event.

If one building encapsulates J+W's approach, it is the Open University Business School completed in 2001. It has a simple H plan with offices in four rectangular wings and shared facilities in the central bar. It exhibits many of J+W's noted features: flat roof, prominent cornice above shadow

gap, white rendered solid walls, strip windows flush with the wall surface and transparent curtain walling. All these elements are crisply detailed with impeccably smooth surfaces, sharp edges and continuous lines, as in the unbroken cornice line.

A straightforward, well mannered building, then. Without being fussy or flashy on the one hand nor puritanically severe on the other, it achieves a certain elegance.

Yet behind this disarmingly straightforward, cool appearance, the Business School manages to pack several powerful punches that only reveal themselves at the edges or are completely hidden. The first of these punches is a pioneering ventilation system in which tempered air circulates through hollow concrete floors, resulting in a consistently comfortable, low-energy building that attained an 'excellent' BREEAM rating. Its second punch comprises

Left to right:
Curtain wall lifted into the third dimension:
New Line Learning Academy, 2010.

Decoration by scientific patterning:
Southampton nanotechnology labs, 2008.

Shimmering iridescent shingles and patterned
curtain wall: Aloft Excel Hotel, 2011.

Overview                                                                    181

a few subtle tweaks that lift the building's appearance.
Externally, these tweaks include ground floor cladding
in rich, mottled orange Corten steel, a slender steel pole
propping up each corner, and screen end walls in slatted
natural timber that permit veiled views into and out of the
staircases. Its third punch is the social interaction that is
deliberately encouraged by the layout. Whereas before,
staff were isolated in cellular offices strung out over a long,
narrow building, they now share facilities in the central bar
and open-plan offices in the wings. As one user posted on
the school's intranet site, "I have talked to more people in a
day than I do in a year."

These three themes of technical innovation, creative
architectonic composition and use of materials, and social
integration underpin most J+W buildings. More than that,
the practice's strengths in these three design aspects
mutually reinforce each other.

Many of J+W's technical innovations tackle building services
and environmental issues. For the conversion in 1999 of a
Grade II listed building into the five-star One Aldwych hotel,
for instance, the practice specified vacuum drainage for the
first time in London. This ploy liberated the bedrooms and
bathrooms from being stacked directly on top of each other,
and the practice harnessed this spatial freedom to win an
award and establish an international reputation overnight in
up-market hotel conversions.

Applying its technical prowess to environmental matters
has pushed the practice to the forefront of sustainable
design, with many of its buildings attaining 'excellent'
BREEAM ratings. Several technical innovations have been
in passive ways of creating the most comfortable internal
environments with the least energy consumption and carbon
emissions. Genuinely passive controls of temperature,
humidity, fresh air and daylight have no gee-whiz gadgetry

**Left and right:**
Net curtain shifted outside external wall:
W Hotel, Leicester Square, 2011.

Elliptical towers evoke the dock's marine
history: Royal Quay, 2005.

to show off. Instead they mould the very shape and fabric of the building. In the Open University the result was a deceptively bland, rectilinear built form. In Housing 21's head office in Beaconsfield completed in 1997, by contrast, the solution was a bold combination of half-vaulted ceiling and central lightwell.

Turning to architectonic composition and style, several inventive devices have been introduced to add texture and vitality to facades that would otherwise remain plain and flat. At New Line Learning Academy in Maidstone completed in 2011, a four-storey high curtain wall has been animated by a syncopated rhythm of six elements: opaque panels in four tones of green, glazed windows and doors, and projecting horizontal louvred sunshades.

At Southampton University's Nanotechnology Research Centre completed in 2008, the curtain wall to the clean room was decorated with endlessly zigzagging white patterns, which are much expanded representations of 'fractal' structures created at the centre by bombarding nanoscale materials with lasers. In this way, the centre's researchers can take pride in their own handiwork embellishing their building. At the same time, J+W defied convention by specifying clear glazing for the curtain wall that offers passers-by glimpses into the clean room and the world-leading research taking place within.

A more kinetic, multicoloured effect was applied at greater expense in 2011 to the flush facade of Aloft Excel Hotel in London Docklands. Here the facade was faced in shingles made out of an American product called Rimex, a textured stainless steel sheet that is given a special acid treatment. Like fish scales, the shingles shimmer and fluctuate between iridescent greens, blues, purples and reds in response to natural changes in daylight. And alongside the steel shingled

Left and right:
Iconic truncated cone: CEAC Cuba,
ongoing.

Hot, spicy, snaking air ducts: Mumbai
Juhu cinema, 2003.

Overview

183

facade, a glazed curtain wall was fritted in intriguing striped patterns that have been compared to a Vasarely painting.

For the W Hotel in Leicester Square, the practice took the understated flush facade one step further than that by bringing in an artist, Jason Bruges, at the start of the project in 2006. The site lay at the heart of the capital's entertainment and theatre district, which is an architectural war zone with new and historic buildings, garish shop fronts and bright lights all fighting for attention in wildly conflicting styles. The team's brainwave here was to move the net curtain that traditionally hangs inside every hotel bedroom window to the outside of the building. During the day, this sheer, translucent outer curtain floats glacially aloof from the area's visual cacophony, unperturbed even by a particularly trashy M&M's World directly below on the ground floor. At night, the whole building wakes up and joins in the throng, as 300 striplights installed behind the veil perform their own

merry dance in changing rainbow colours, replaying scenes of the surrounding cityscape captured by time-lapsed photography earlier in the day. And on the practical side, the highly visual outer screen even improves the environmental performance of the building.

Moving on from facades to overall building form, not all J+W buildings are rectilinear. A few are lifted by more sculptural effects, as in the concave and convex forms of Aloft Excel Hotel. At Royal Quay one mile further east, three prominent apartment blocks that rise out of the water have been shaped into eye-catching ellipses with a suitably marine theme.

Even more exotic—iconic even—is the reception building to Cuba's new microbiology research complex, currently under construction. Its lecture theatre is shaped like a truncated cone that is clad in vivid orange mosaic and erupts through the floating roof canopy.

Left and right:
Dwellings and business units combined
under one roof: Bruges Place, 1986.

Hotel guests welcomed by lobby culture:
Hilton London Tower Bridge, 2006.

However, if J+W's architecture is inclined towards plain, cool pragmatism, then the establishment of the practice's in-house interior design studio in 1995 has boosted many buildings, particularly hotels and cinemas, into exuberant, theatrical spectacles. At Mumbai's Juhu cinema completed in 2003, for instance, excitement galore comes from snaking air ducts in hot, spicy colours inspired by Indian saris and curries, along with white air inlets resembling fish eyes. Note that the interior design here is expressed in the services engineer's air ducts: a cross-over of disciplines that would have been much harder to achieve if interior designer and architect did not belong to the same practice.

Theatre only comes to life when people enter, and many J+W buildings have been deliberately configured to enhance the experience of occupying, visiting and working in them, and to encourage social interaction. As we have seen at the Open University, the new Business School offers plenty of opportunity for chance encounters where staff can chat and share ideas. Bruges Place in London completed in 1986 overturned town planning conventions by combining dwellings and business premises within the same shell, inaugurating the new live-work building type.

The conversion of One Aldwych hotel opened the practice's eyes to the potentials of 'lobby culture', where guests are encouraged to do what comes naturally, which is to relax near the main entrance and watch the world go by. In the Hilton London Tower Bridge, completed in 2006, much of the ground floor was given over to a comfortable lounge that has views over a pedestrian plaza lying just outside the window wall. Guests are invited to wander freely without negotiating any obstructing doors into the adjacent dining room or up an open staircase to their bedroom floor.

**Left and right:**
Caring/sharing communal spaces for
young and old: Darwin Court, 2001.

The school that kids can't tear
themselves away from: Passmores
Academy, 2011.

The practice has even transposed this lobby culture to accommodation for ageing people and public-sector schools. At Darwin Court, a new "community for the third age" completed in 2001, the communal sitting room and dining room flow into each other, with the building's main circulation route passing openly between them. So welcoming and friendly is this building that grandchildren now want to come and see their grandparents rather than the other way round. In several ways, Darwin Court helps its ageing occupants retain their stake in the wider community and is held up as an exemplar across Europe.

Passmores Academy in Harlow, Essex, revolves around a large, vibrant 'heartspace', or toplit atrium, where all 1,200 pupils circulate, take refreshments and mix with their schoolmates without fear of bullying. "The kids love the building", says headteacher Vic Goddard. "It's got real warmth to the place. We can't kick the kids out at the end of the day. The canteen is open from 7.30 am to 4.50 at night. At five o'clock at night, they'll still be here sitting over a hot chocolate."

These 14 examples, along with over 160 awards and commendations won over the years by the practice, demonstrate an architecture practice working proficiently on several levels. For a start, J+W can be relied on to deliver mainstream buildings, such as public-sector housing and schools, on limited budgets that are nevertheless very serviceable, highly sustainable and inspiring. In several buildings, such as Juhu cinema, the partnership of architects and interior designers adds an exciting theatricality, while it enlivens accommodation for the elderly, schools and hotels with a lobby culture that encourages social interaction. And in some occasions, as in Cuba or W Hotel, it can even pull an architectural icon out of the hat.

What more can you ask of an architect?

# Index

**14 Stephenson Way**
Jestico + Whiles developed their first
office/ studio in Euston, winning an RIBA
Award for architecture in 1990 and an IDI
interior design award in 1991.

# Thank you

When Duncan McCorquodale and Kate Trant walked through the front door we knew not what to expect. Now, after a year, we should like to thank Artifice books on architecture for inviting us to join them, David Taylor, Martin Spring and Peter Murray for undertaking a very enjoyable period of reflection on 35 years of practice. A review we had not planned but another example of happenstance, as we say in the book, that has led the practice to new experiences through its life.

And it is precisely everyone who has walked through our doors, be it colleagues, clients or consultants that we should like to sincerely thank for making Jestico + Whiles what it is, a 'we' practice, not an 'I' practice.

It is not only people but buildings that have been important in creating the spirit of place for the practice. Whether it was our first office at 53 Endell Street in Covent Garden, or the brilliant top floor furrier's workshop by St Paul's in the City, the extraordinary discovery of the Stephenson Way building in Euston to our present beautiful Cobourg Street, the last original building of Euston Station and then, of course, Prague, all have been wonderful places to work in and party in.

And so, a big thank you to everyone from all over the world who has worked with us, everyone who has shared the good times and the bad times with us, and everyone who has contributed to the practice's success.

# Image credits

We should like to thank all the photographers of our work for the incredible care and patience they have taken to record the buildings in the best possible way. And whilst we believe we have credited all the colleagues with whom we have worked, we should like to apologise for any unintentional omission from the list: Radovan Bocek, David Churchill, Peter Cook, Tim Crocker, Reto Halme, Hufton + Crowe, Aleš Jungmann, Benedict Luxmore, James Morris, Gerry O'Leary, John Peck, Paul Ratigan, Jo Reid, Philip Sayer, Timothy Soar, Aurélien Thomas, John Whiles and Charlotte Wood.

# Colophon

Artifice books on architecture
10a Acton Street
London WC1X 9NG
United Kingdom

Tel: +44 (0)20 7713 5097
Fax: +44 (0)20 7713 8682
sales@artificebooksonline.com
www.artificebooksonline.com

All opinions expressed within this publication are those of the authors and not necessarily of the publisher.

British Library Cataloguing-in-Publication Data. A CIP record for this book is available from the British Library.

ISBN 978 1 908967 12 1

Designed by Alex Wright and Elin Svensson.

Artifice books on architecture is an environmentally responsible company. *PLUS* is printed on sustainably sourced paper.